National Union of Teachers

CAMBRIDGE SOUVENIR

T0364323

COUNCILLOR E. W. AMIES, J.P.
Mayor of Cambridge

National Union of Teachers Conference

CAMBRIDGE SOUVENIR

EASTER, 1928

Printed for the Conference at

THE UNIVERSITY PRESS
CAMBRIDGE

CAMBRIDGE
UNIVERSITY PRESS

University Printing House, Cambridge CB2 8BS, United Kingdom

Cambridge University Press is part of the University of Cambridge.

It furthers the University's mission by disseminating knowledge in the pursuit of education, learning and research at the highest international levels of excellence.

www.cambridge.org
Information on this title: www.cambridge.org/9781107494435

© Cambridge University Press 1928

First published 1928
First paperback edition 2015

A catalogue record for this publication is available from the British Library

ISBN 978-1-107-49443-5 Paperback

Phot: Elliott & Fry

W. W. HILL, B.Sc.
President of the N. U. T.

PREFACE

The Press Committee of the Cambridge Conference Council desire to express gratitude to all who have assisted in the production of the Souvenir:

to the writers of the articles;

to the Syndics of the University Press for the exceedingly generous act of undertaking the publication of the Souvenir;

to Mr G. V. Carey, M.A., the Educational Secretary at the University Press, for kindness and courteous help given during the preparation of the volume.

J. D. LIVINGSTONE
Hon. Secretary of the Press Committee

F. MANDER, B.Sc.
Ex-President of the N.U.T.

CONTENTS

MRS LEAH MANNING, J.P.
"Our Executive Member"

J. HOLT, M.A.
Conference Secretary

W. G. POINTS, M.A.
Chairman of the Conference Council

ILLUSTRATIONS

For the portrait of the Mayor on p. ii, we are indebted to *The Cambridge Chronicle* for the loan of a block.

The illustrations on pp. 5, 16, 17, 19, 33, 35, 45, 49, 53, 54, 60, 75, 77, 81 are from photographs by Messrs Frith and Co., Ltd., Reigate; that on p. 14 from a photograph by J. Palmer Clarke, Cambridge; that on p. 59 from a photograph by Mr E. Clennett.

The Rev. G. A. WEEKES, M.A.
*Master of Sidney Sussex College and Vice-Chancellor
of the University*

FOREWORD

by the Rev. G. A. WEEKES, M.A.
Vice-Chancellor of the University

THE visit of the National Union of Teachers to Cambridge falls in the quiet of the Easter Vacation, when not an undergraduate is to be seen passing through the College courts or into the laboratories and lecture-rooms. To the dons vacation is a welcome time of rest from the labour of teaching and the ever-growing work of administration, and for comparatively unhindered study and research; but in Easter week even the dons claim a holiday.

But Cambridge Town has no vacations. In the University, men may come and men may go, but the motor coaches, which link up scores of scattered villages with Cambridge, still bring their hundreds into the town, farmers and traders, buyers and sellers; and the tourists are always with us, passing through in a steady stream. If the streets are less animated—how could it be otherwise in the absence of some five thousand lively young men and women?—yet they are not exactly empty. In Sidney Street or Petty Cury it is well to look both ways before crossing the street.

When they reach Cambridge, not a few of the Delegates will be on familiar ground. They will need no guide, but will just wander round in spare half-hours revisiting well-remembered spots, and noting, with approval or otherwise, changes and additions. Those who visit the town for the first time will find in this *Souvenir* the best of guide-books. But even those who already know their Cambridge will find much to interest them in this book, whether their tastes are historical, or antiquarian, or they are mainly concerned with the progress of education in the country.

The purpose of a foreword, as I understand it, is to call attention to the value and the interest of the articles which have been contributed by skilled and learned writers. If the sun shines on the meeting, as we all hope, its members will carry away with them, together with the more serious impressions of an important conference, a memory of quiet beauty which few other towns in England can give.

THE UNIVERSITY OF CAMBRIDGE

by C. J. B. Gaskoin, M.A.

I. *UNIVERSITAS CANTABRIGIENSIS*

Those who have seen in other towns or cities imposing buildings called "The University" will seek in vain to find their like in Cambridge. A University, indeed, there is—the University of Cambridge, or (in older phrase) the Cantabrigian University. And to the yet more ancient town this ancient University has brought its world-wide fame. The University, too, is something else than the group of Colleges, Halls, Hostels, Houses, and other bodies between which its members are, or used to be, divided. Identified with none, at once more and less than all of them together, it has and has ever had in its own right whatever possessions, powers, laws, duties, and authorities have belonged to it —Schools, Senate House, Museums, or other buildings; houses and lands; Statutes and Ordinances; Council, Senate, House of Regents; Chancellor, Vice-Chancellor, Proctors, and Bedells. And, though in age no "University" building can vie with the oldest of the college structures, the University itself is older and greater than any other institution of academic Cambridge. For it dates back to the time when students and teachers gathered in the town were first numerous and considerable enough to receive from Authority recognition as a "Universitas", that is, a body or guild of men bound together, like members of a Merchant or Craft Guild, by common aims and interests, and worthy, like them, of rights and privileges established to secure their ends.

The University is, in fact, neither a building nor a group of buildings, neither a single college nor a group of colleges, but the whole body of teachers and students of Cambridge, organised and privileged, under the authority of their Chancellor, for the advancement of sound Religion and Learning.

II. BEGINNINGS

The birth of the University, if the date of that obscure event could be ascertained, would probably be found not far before or after the opening of the thirteenth century. In 1209 some of the riotous students expelled by King John from Oxford came to Cambridge, while others went to Northampton or elsewhere; and perhaps what brought them was the fame of a school or teacher of which history as yet knows nothing, but which kept some still here when the rest went back. At any rate, ever after, if not before, scholars came to Cambridge to be so trained (it is thus that the Bidding Prayer defines the purpose of the University) "that there may never be wanting a succession of just persons, duly qualified for the service of God in Church and State". But of the justice of scholars and teachers alike Cambridge townsfolk were for many centuries very imperfectly convinced.

For the students, coming from England—especially the North and East, from Ireland, Scotland, and Wales, and possibly from countries yet farther off, and fighting each other, after their kind, as in great battles between "North" and "South," would at any moment join their rival bands to war upon the townsmen in fights whose faint echoes sounded still in "town and gown" combats a generation or two ago. And their seniors from an early date asserted, with the backing of royal officials, privileges and jurisdictions making it impossible for the men of Cambridge to be, as all medieval townsmen would be, masters in their own house. The national interest of learning was supported by Authority against the local interest of town autonomy, even if its more violent defenders could not always claim the King's countenance. So, though all students were for many generations "Clerks in Holy Orders" in some degree, holiness was perhaps the last characteristic ascribed to them, as a class, by Cambridge townsmen.

More grievous even, perhaps, because more ever-pressing, than the University's claim to judge cases in which its members were involved, must have been its claim to demand for its members board and housing upon reasonable terms. "Reason" is apt to mean different things to seller and buyer, and no doubt Cambridge bakers and brewers hotly resented the fixing of their prices by persons not even engaged in other trades within the town. And even greater was the townsmen's wrath when Masters of Arts, with the Chancellor's sanction, compelled landlords to accept them as tenants, that they might be principals of a "hostel" for the lodging of scholars, or even to promise them the succession to the present occupier. But quarrels on this matter did not endure for ever, for soon, slowly but surely, the college system was built up, and, when the colleges took in not only endowed scholars but "pensioners", or paying students, the lodging problem faded away, till the vast increase in numbers revived it in a milder form for the nineteenth century.

III. COLLEGES

In many ways the third quarter of the thirteenth century ushers in a time of beginnings, an age of transition from the Middle Ages proper, through the "Later Middle Ages", to the Modern Age of the Renaissance and the Reformation. And this was so in the English Universities. For the time from Henry III to Edward III forms the first great period of college-making, by the University itself or—a far more common and lasting method—by pious founders and benefactors of all ranks.

At Cambridge in the early days of Edward III the University possessed a "University Hall" and a "University Hostel". But such townhouses taken over by University authorities were destined to give place to new halls or colleges, built expressly, by royal or private munificence, to accommodate scholars. University Hall was soon swallowed up in the Countess of Clare's "Clare Hall", University Hostel in the Countess of Pembroke's "Pembroke Hall"—two foundations which centuries later preferred to "Hall" the more fashionable style of "College". And Clare itself had a predecessor in its own kind. For the ancient House of Peter, starting, more than half a century earlier, with two houses endowed by a Bishop of Ely for scholar-clerks he had previously quartered on the Brethren of the Hospital of St

PETERHOUSE

John (to their great and mutual dissatisfaction),
had soon begun to grow into the new-built college
of Peterhouse. Meanwhile a Bishop had founded
"Michaelhouse" and a King "King's Hall". And
now Pembroke Hall was quickly followed by
Trinity Hall, Corpus Christi College, and "Gonville Hall" (our Gonville and Caius College). And
Corpus (marvel of marvels!) was actually founded
by two Guilds of Cambridge town: perhaps the
dreadful horror of the recent Black Death for a
time stilled ancient feuds and incited town and
gown alike to pious enterprises.

IV. MORE COLLEGES

For nearly another century no great new foundation was established. But the University itself
was at last rearing buildings of its own—"Schools",
which then included, and are now included in, the
University Library; and the planting of "Buckingham House" in Cambridge by Benedictine Monks
in 1419 formed a link with the next great period
of college-making. For the assignment of this
house to his new Magdalene College by Audley,
least worthy of all Cambridge founders, after the
Dissolution of the Monasteries, illustrated, though
on a paltry scale, a characteristic of University
development for a hundred years before—the
conversion to the new collegiate purpose of en-
dowments originally monastic. Only St Catharine's, of all the colleges founded between 1441
and 1546, with the Royal Foundations of King's
and Trinity at either end, was neither originally
dowered nor afterwards enriched with monastic
possessions; Queens', Christ's, and St John's—

owing much, like Clare and Pembroke, to noble ladies—followed the fashion; and Bishop Alcock grafted Jesus College on to the decaying and deserted nunnery of St Radegund, saving for all time some of the oldest and most beautiful things in college architecture.

King's, sweeping away town dwellings to clear a site that for centuries it could not fill, and marking itself off from the University as an exclusive and privileged corporation, dwelt for centuries apart, a beautiful but haughty stranger, till in the nineteenth century it made a splendid sacrifice to join in friendly fellowship with other foundations. Henry VIII's magnificent college, on the other hand, absorbing Michaelhouse and King's Hall, became in time so famous that not long ago uninstructed foreigners sometimes believed "Trinity, Cambridge" to be another name for the University itself.

Later foundations were few and far between. Emmanuel and Sidney Sussex under Elizabeth witnessed to a real if narrow zeal for the Reformation. In the next two centuries benefactors generally endowed Fellowships or Scholarships, or erected not new colleges but new college buildings. Then came Downing (first occupied in 1821, though planned more than a hundred years before), the only "open" college of its century. Selwyn (1882) was founded solely for members of the Church of England, though with no such narrow exclusiveness as marked the Puritan colleges in their early days. Fitzwilliam House (1887), enrolling now all but a fraction of the so-called "Non-Collegiate Students" (1869), assures to them, with the full sanction and support of the

University, that corporate, essentially "collegiate", life without which no man can hope to get the full benefit of a Cambridge career. And still outside the University—though their members may sit on its Boards, lecture in its Schools, examine in its Triposes, and even, in "title", take its degrees—stand the women's colleges of Girton (1872) and Newnham (1875).

There the catalogue ends, for the twentieth century has as yet founded no new college, though new college buildings, training colleges for clergy of different churches, and—above all—great University Museums, Laboratories, and Schools have displaced business premises and private houses, and college gardens and grounds.

V. THE INNER LIFE

With these external changes in successive centuries have gone changes also in the inner life of the University.

The medieval students who filled lodgings, hostels, and early colleges, and fought their hosts or foes, were generally either ordained or contemplating ordination, and their studies, though not merely theological, never went beyond the traditional curriculum, with Divinity and Canon Law predominating. But colleges endowed with monastic lands were founded mainly in the age of the Renaissance and the Reformation, when old barriers were breaking down and new worlds coming to light through intellectual as well as geographical exploration; when new studies and doctrines were creeping into Cambridge Schools; when Erasmus read Greek in the new Queens'

College, or the White Horse Inn (between King's College and the Bull Hotel) was furtively haunted by admirers of Luther; and from the enlarged, enriched, enlightened University sprang a race of men renowned in Tudor and early Stuart days in science or letters, in Church or State.

The Puritan colleges arose in a Cambridge where Dr Caius had to bewail the tearing and cutting to pieces of "all the ornaments" of his college by the Vice-Chancellor himself, "with horrible names and epithets"—where Whitgift, Master of Trinity, deposed the Lady Margaret Reader who helped to write an "Admonition to Parliament" attacking the Prayer Book as "an unperfect book" culled out of a "popish dunghill ...full of all abominations"—where Dr Cheke of Peterhouse dared to tell the University in Great St Mary's that Satan himself invented bishops, archbishops, metropolitans, patriarchs, and—finally—the Pope.

The long, comparatively changeless period that preluded the strenuous nineteenth century saw a loyally Anglican Cambridge, planted in a sternly Puritan land, pass through the tribulation of Civil War, Commonwealth, and Protectorate to the Happy Restoration, only to find in James II a new oppressor, and turn disgustedly, after his fall, to earn a lasting repute for a new loyalty to Hanoverians and Whigs. And then, despite new Professorships in Science and Mathematics created in the "curious" later Stuart age, with others following in their wake, despite the great figures of Newton, Bentley, Law, and Paley, came the intellectual torpor and moral decline. From this, late in the eighteenth century, new men, new causes, new inspirations, new enthusiams—Pitt, Emancipation, the Evangelical Movement, the hopes of 1789—awoke the sleepers, and the nineteenth century saw a new generation of Cambridge men famous in almost every walk of life.

Then, with Science triumphing in the intellectual world and Democracy advancing in politics, expansion and "Reform" came to the Universities also. By the Statutes of successive Royal Commissions, by her own repeated efforts to put her house in better order, Cambridge grew so transmuted that, but for her ancient buildings, a Cambridge man of the year of Waterloo would hardly have recognised his Alma Mater in the University that sent hundreds and thousands to fight and toil for their country through the Great War, while dull, hard, disheartening work fell to a few left behind, who "kept things going" for the handful of war-time students and prepared for the vast inrush that the peace must bring.

Matriculations are now more than four times as numerous as they were a century ago. There are seven times as many Triposes. To the twenty-two Professors have been added thirty-five more, besides twenty-four Readers, and Lecturers innumerable. The vastly increased expenditure has forced the University to accept an annual Government grant, bringing in its train yet more reorganisation, under new Statutes prepared by yet another Royal Commission. Meanwhile, with brilliant success, the co-operation of both central and local governmental authorities with the University in another direction has given the "poor scholar"—always the special care of University benefactors—opportunities far greater, even, than he enjoyed before. By ever-extending "Extra-mural" work—"University Extension" and the like—the University is helping to raise the standard of teaching outside its walls to the high level expected within them. And through its own "Local Examinations", and others conducted for many Government or educational authorities, it is testing and helping to guide education in remote portions of the Empire, and sometimes, even, in the world outside.

THE COLLEGES OF CAMBRIDGE

by S. C. ROBERTS, M.A.

Secretary to the Syndics of the University Press

THE colleges of Cambridge may be considered
from various points of view—geographical. historical, architectural. Geographically, their posi-
tions are for the most part haphazard. They were
built before the days of town-planning, sometimes
on the site of an older religious house, sometimes
on a main street which has now become an obscure lane, sometimes on a more spacious site
from which shops and houses and inns had been
cleared for the purpose. Each college is the result
of a separate foundation and each was built as
a unit, with little or no reference to its sister-
foundations.

Yet, historically, the University comes first.
The first college was founded with a view to the
better ordering of the student's life at the end of
the thirteenth century, and every century, except
the present, has witnessed new foundations.
Architecturally, therefore, the colleges are a
glorious medley. Every style of English architecture, in a form pure or debased, may be studied
within their walls.

It is doubly convenient to begin with PETER-
HOUSE: it is the oldest foundation and it is the
first college that the traveller sees if he enters
Cambridge by the Trumpington Road. Founded
by Hugh de Balsham in 1284, it retains
little of its original buildings save the entrance-
doorways to the Hall. The Chapel, built in

the seventeenth century, stands in the middle of the court and is joined to the buildings on either side by galleries. On the north side is a set of famous rooms where the poet Gray lived in the eighteenth century. He was more than usually afraid of fire and bought a long rope to be used in emergencies. Two lively members of the college, knowing Gray's weakness, raised a false alarm; Gray slid down the rope and found himself, according to the common story, in a tub of cold water. The bar from which the rope was hung may still be seen. Nor should the traveller leave Peterhouse without seeing its deer-park—the only one in Cambridge.

On the opposite side of the road is PEMBROKE, whither Gray migrated after his ill-treatment at Peterhouse. Pembroke, founded in 1347 by the Lady Mary de Valence, Countess of Pembroke, can boast of other poets besides Gray: Spenser, with whose name a mulberry-tree in the college garden is still associated; Gabriel Harvey, the friend of Spenser; Crashaw, "poet and saint" of the seventeenth century; Mason, the friend of Gray; and Christopher Smart, the author of the *Song to David*. Nineteenth-century architectural enthusiasm has left a heavy mark upon Pembroke, but its Chapel represents the first work of Sir Christopher Wren and was built at the expense of Matthew Wren, Bishop of Ely. Pembroke was, indeed, as famous for its bishops and martyrs as for its poets; among them were Ridley, Bradford, Whitgift, and Andrewes. The younger Pitt entered the college in 1773.

Further along the street is CORPUS CHRISTI, founded in 1352. In the Old Court of Corpus is seen the best complete specimen of a medieval college court. The Hall belongs to the early nineteenth century, but on three sides of the court the fourteenth-century rooms and staircases remain. Corpus has one of the most famous libraries in

QUEENS' COLLEGE, CLOISTER COURT

the world; it was bequeathed to the college by Matthew Parker, who was Master from 1544 to 1553, and contains an Anglo-Saxon version of the Gospels and many other treasures.

Opposite Corpus is ST CATHARINE'S, founded in 1473. It consists of a single court of red brick, of which the fourth side was never built. The college is thus open to the street, but originally it was built to face the other way and its front is actually in Queens' Lane, which was once the main artery of the town. Queens' Lane takes its name from the college which stands opposite the old front of St Catharine's. Founded in 1446, it commemorates two queens of England—Margaret, wife of Henry VI, and Elizabeth Woodville, wife of Edward IV. Hidden away from the main line of traffic, QUEENS' is one of the architectural glories of Cambridge. Its first court, fortunately little altered in the course of centuries, is a splendid example of Tudor brickwork, and the second, or Cloister, court is even more beautiful by reason not only of its cloistered neatness but of the fine half-timbered gallery, belonging to the President's Lodge, which runs along the top of one of the cloisters. One of the turrets in the corner of the first court is still known as Erasmus Tower, for here the great Renaissance scholar worked when he came to teach Greek in the University about 1510.

From Queens' Lane there is a side-entrance to KING'S COLLEGE, the foundation of Henry VI. It was planned on a royal scale, but the only part of Henry's design which was completed was the famous chapel. Nearly 300 feet long and 90 feet high, this chapel is the supreme triumph of the Perpendicular style.

The stained glass windows are worthy of their setting, and an afternoon service, with no other light than that of candles, is one of the experiences that old Cambridge men remember long after a hundred details of University life are forgotten. Life at King's has been recorded by many novelists —Mr E. F. Benson, Mr E. M. Forster, and Mr Shane Leslie; and one of Rupert Brooke's best

KING'S COLLEGE CHAPEL

known poems, *The Old Vicarage, Grantchester*, was written for a King's College magazine. From the west end of the Chapel one looks across the most spacious lawn in Cambridge. At the bottom is the river and on the right is CLARE, a jewel of Renaissance architecture.

CLARE COLLEGE AND BRIDGE

In date of foundation (1326) Clare comes next to Peterhouse, but its building belongs to the seventeenth century. Clare has a beautiful bridge, and beyond it and beyond the "Backs" is a new part of the College, opened in 1925; within the entrance-gateway are commemorated the names of the Clare men who fell in the War and the building is named the Memorial Building. One of the early worthies of Clare was Hugh Latimer, who preached his famous "Sermons on the Card" in St Edward's Church.

Next to Clare is TRINITY HALL, founded in 1350; it is a college famous for its library, which remains as it was built about the end of Elizabeth's reign and can still show some chained books; for its lawyers, from Stephen Gardiner, "the great instrument of Henry VIII", to Mr Augustine Birrell; and for its oarsmen, among whom have been numbered Mr Reginald McKenna and Mr Stanley Bruce, Prime Minister of Australia.

The name of GONVILLE AND CAIUS COLLEGE commemorates two founders: Edmund Gonville, a Norfolk clergyman who founded Gonville Hall in 1347, and John Caius, who re-founded his old college as Gonville and Caius in 1557. Caius was a famous doctor, being Physician to both Edward VI and Mary, and his college has preserved the medical tradition which he established. Caius made many benefactions to his college, and his memory is preserved, in particular, by the three gates which he built: the entrance-gate, which was the Gate of Humility; the gate leading to the inner court, which was the Gate of Virtue; and the gate leading out of the college to the Schools, which was the Gate of Honour. This last gate is one of the most beautiful pieces of Renaissance work in Cambridge. Dr Perse, founder of the Perse School, was also a Caius man and a great benefactor to his college as well as to the town.

The greatest of all collegiate foundations is TRINITY. It was founded in 1546, with provision for a Master and sixty Fellows, by Henry VIII, and it absorbed three smaller hostels. Some small portions of these remain, but the magnificence of

Great Court is mainly due to Thomas Nevile, a Pembroke man who became Master of Trinity in 1593. Nevile also planned the court, which bears his name, on the other side of the Hall. Here are massive cloisters on either side and the noble library built by Sir Christopher Wren at the

TRINITY COLLEGE LIBRARY

further end. Within the library are many treasures—first folios of Shakespeare, the manuscripts of *Lycidas*, *In Memoriam*, *Esmond*, and many others.

For Trinity abounds in famous men. One staircase, just on the right of the Great Gate, is associated with the names of Newton, Thackeray, and Macaulay. In the Chapel are statues of Bacon, Barrow, Whewell, Tennyson; also of Macaulay and Newton. It was of the last that Wordsworth wrote:

> The antechapel where the statue stood
> Of Newton with his prism and silent face,
> The marble index of a mind for ever
> Voyaging through strange seas of thought alone.

Hard by Trinity is the college that once surpassed it in numbers—ST JOHN'S, founded under the will of the Lady Margaret, Countess of Richmond and mother of Henry VII, in 1511. The first two courts of St John's are, like those of Queens', magnificent examples of Tudor brickwork. The First Court has suffered by the destruction of its northern side, but the Second remains intact and contains, on one of its upper floors, the most beautiful room in Cambridge—the Combination Room (originally the Master's Gallery) nearly 100 feet long with panelled walls and a fine plaster ceiling (see p. 59). Beyond the Second Court is a third, which leads to the river, and on the other side of the river is a pretentious pile of neo-Gothic buildings built in the early nineteenth century. Joining the new with the old is the famous "Bridge of Sighs", but more beautiful is the Old Bridge built at the end of the seventeenth century. St John's has been the nursing-ground of statesmen in several centuries—Burghley, Strafford, and Palmerston were Johnians. Poets, too, have flourished there, among them Matthew Prior and Wordsworth. It was Wordsworth who

> could not print
> Ground where the grass had yielded to the steps
> Of generations of illustrious men,
> Unmoved....

Off the main track is MAGDALENE, the only ancient college on the further side of the Cam. It was founded in 1542 on the site of a Benedictine house and is famous as the college of Samuel Pepys, whose library, including the manuscript of his *Diary*, was bequeathed to the college and remains exactly as he left it, every book in its original case and in its proper place. Charles Kingsley was a Magdalene man, and Arthur Christopher Benson, who made a certain "College Window" almost as famous as the Pepysian Library, was Master from 1915 to his death in 1925.

JESUS COLLEGE is uniquely fortunate in standing in its own grounds. Its playing-fields lie between the college buildings and the river and it is fitting that Jesus should be a famous rowing college. Founded in 1497 on the site of the Priory of St Radegund, it preserves, in many details, the plan of a medieval monastery. The Chapel and cloisters, though now in part restored, remain as when they formed part of the old monastic building. Other notable features of Jesus are the fine entrance-gateway of brick and the walled passage (commonly known as the "Chimney") which leads to it. Jesus is associated with two famous names in literature—those of Sterne and Coleridge.

SIDNEY SUSSEX COLLEGE, founded in 1596, was also built on the site of a Franciscan Friary, but nothing of the old building remains. Sidney was Oliver Cromwell's college and in the Hall may be seen his portrait, "with pimples, warts and everything". The Chapel of Sidney, recently enlarged and rebuilt in the Renaissance style, is one of the most noteworthy modern buildings in Cambridge.

The Lady Margaret, who founded St John's,

was also the foundress of CHRIST'S COLLEGE (1505). It is a college famous for its gardens and the gardens are famous for "Milton's mulberry-tree"; for Milton came up to Christ's in 1625 and, in his own words, found "more than ordinary respect at the hands of those courteous and learned men, the Fellows". Several of his poems were written while he was at Cambridge, and *Lycidas* was first printed at the University Press in 1638. Christ's was also the college of Charles Darwin.

EMMANUEL COLLEGE, "the pure house of Emmanuel", was founded in 1584 by Sir Walter Mildmay. It was built on the site of an old Dominican house and its first Chapel (now the library) was built to run north and south. After the Civil War, however, Sir Christopher Wren was engaged to build a new Chapel at the end of the First Court in a position similar to that of Peterhouse. Inside the Chapel is a tablet which records how an Emmanuel man, John Harvard, emigrated to Massachusetts and "there dying in 1638 bequeathed to a college newly established... his library and one half of his estate". Harvard men accordingly look upon Emmanuel as "Alma Grandmater".

Last of the old colleges comes DOWNING, founded under the will of Sir George Downing in 1800. Only a portion of the plan for the large quadrangle was carried out, but the architects of the future will no doubt have their opportunity.

SELWYN COLLEGE, a Church of England foundation, was established in memory of Bishop George Augustus Selwyn in 1882, and the nineteenth century also saw the growth of the two women's colleges—GIRTON and NEWNHAM.

Student life in Cambridge has undergone many changes since Hugh de Balsham established his scholars in Peterhouse in 1284; but college spirit and college tradition persist through every phase of external change. For every Cambridge man the college is the focus of his affection and his loyalty.

CUSTOMS AND COSTUMES

by The Rev. Canon H. P. STOKES,
LL.D., LITT.D., F.S.A.

THE date of the origin of the University of Cambridge is uncertain—if indeed there was ever any formal inauguration. There were undoubtedly students here at the beginning of the fourteenth century, and more than six hundred years ago, in the year 1325, a Chancellor of the University incidentally appears in connection with a certain Archdeacon and with an official of Barnwell Priory; again a few years later another head of our University was appointed by the Pope to adjudicate in an important case. The Chancellor at that date, and for long afterwards, seems to have held office for a year; but early in the sixteenth century the celebrated Bishop Fisher was re-elected for some years, and afterwards the holder of the high office was appointed for life. It may be noted that of the first eight of these great Chancellors six perished on the scaffold. Former holders of the office had been personal leaders in the work of the University; but now a resident Vice-Chancellor was at the head of the practical teaching.

The dress of the Chancellors in those early days—like that of the Masters of Arts—was closely allied to the ordinary clerical costume of the times. The statutes of Peterhouse, the earliest of the colleges, required that "a Fellow should always appear in the University dressed in the proper robes (*vestes*) of a scholar"; and so for the members of the various hostels then in existence.

Besides the Masters of Arts, there were "Masters in Grammar". Their rank was inferior, but they were elaborately appointed. The quaint ceremonies at the creation of a "M. Gram.", *ferulâ et virgis*, may be quoted:

"Whan the Father hath arguyde as shall plese the Proctour, the Bedyll in Arte shall bring the Master of Gramer to the Vice-Chauncelar, delyvering him a Palmer wyᵗʰ a Rodde, which the Vice-Chauncelar shall gyve to the seyde Master in Gramer, & so create hym Master. Then shall the Bedell purvay for every Master in Gramer a shrewde Boy, whom the Master in Gramer shall bete openlye in the Scolys, and the Master in Gramer shall give the Boye a Grote for hys Labour, & another Grote to hym that provydeth the Rode, and the Palma &c. de singulis. And thus endythe the Acte in that Facultye."

The degree of "M. Gram.", however, was not largely taken, and in the middle of the sixteenth century it fell out of use.

It is only possible in this short article to mention a few of the customs and costumes of the University, past and present. Reference must of course be made to a University office which has existed from the first, and still holds its picturesque career. The *Bedells* were not originally graduates of the University; but they were always helpful officials. Of old many of the scholars were poor and needy, whilst some of the Bedells were well-to-do. It is to their honour that a long list of them may be found among the Benefactors of the University. Afterwards the office was given to graduates, and the title of *Esquire Bedells* has for centuries been held by Masters of Arts of position.

An early seal gives an interesting representation

AN ESQUIRE BEDELL (1815) WITH A YEOMAN BEDELL

of an old Bedell, holding a simple staff. Later on, silver maces were presented by the Chancellors, and are still, in scholastic processions, borne in solemn state. Formerly there were three Esquire Bedells—one of Divinity (or Civil Law), one of Arts, and "the other Bedell"; but about 65 years ago the office of the last-mentioned ceased. An inferior officer (the Yeoman Bedell or "the Dog Bedell") of old existed, and the post has lately been revived.

Another set of officers of great importance has existed from the earliest times, the *Proctors*, two of whom are annually chosen by the colleges in a certain rotation. Their insignia were a linstock and a halberd respectively; they wear their hoods "squared", as a ruff. They carry books, sometimes supposed to be Bibles but really copies of the University Statutes. They are attended by picturesque servants, or constables, popularly known as "Bull-dogs". The Proctors figure prominently at all public functions; they patrol the streets at night, exercising control over the undergraduates, and have the power of inflicting fines for certain offences. The Duke of York awhile back laughingly referred to the 6*s.* 8*d.* of which he was mulcted when *in statu pupillari*. There has lately been added a University official to supervise the motor traffic of undergraduates.

The *Public Orator* is another prominent official at Senate House functions. He introduces, with a Latin speech, those who are presented for honorary degrees. The late Orator, Sir John Sandys, published a volume of such elegant effusions; and the present Orator's speeches are noted for their wit and poetical fancy.

The Senate House is again and again crowded with the students who are introduced to the Vice-Chancellor, by their college "Fathers", for their degrees—those who have passed in honours, and those who have taken the ordinary "poll" examinations. "Triposes," as the higher examinations are called, were formerly chiefly mathematical honours. To these, classical lists were added a little more than 100 years ago, and now almost every subject has its list.

The first name in the Mathematical Tripos was of old called the Senior Wrangler, and the holder of this distinguished position was presented with peculiar honour, while the last in order in the third class (or *junior optimes*)—popularly known as "the Wooden Spoon"—received an effusive reception. But the classes are now printed in alphabetical order, and the public *éclat* is quieter and the fun of the fair has ceased.

As remarked above, the original dress of the Masters and of the students was somewhat similar to the ordinary clerical attire. Later on variation was introduced, sometimes special and even fantastic; for instance, John Skelton, the poet, who was a graduate at both Universities, when he received a special honour here in 1504/5, "used the dress allowed him by the Prince, in white and green, on which was embroidered the word CALLIOPE". At times, as we read from a complaint made to Archbishop Laud in 1636, some of the Cambridge "undergraduates wore ye new fashioned gowns of any colour whatsoever, blue or green, or red or mixt, without any uniformity but in hanging sleeves".

In the next century, the noblemen and the

ADMISSION OF THE SENIOR WRANGLER IN 1842

Fellow-Commoners made a brave show in their elaborate gowns—see for instance the fine picture of Lord Byron prefixed to Elze's *Life* of that poet.

But these glories are a thing of the past; the gowns of the undergraduates are simpler, such as the blue gowns of Trinity and Caius, the black gown of Clare with its chevron of velvet, the thick parallel bars of St John's, the long velvet stripes of Corpus, and so on; and only the Doctors in their scarlet enliven the processions and assemblies: as to these, while formerly they were limited to the old faculties of Divinity, Law, and Medicine, now, in addition to the resplendent robe of the Doctors of Music, there are many new gowns representing the newer faculties, including the quaint red stripes of the modern Ph.D.s.

WOMEN STUDENTS IN CAMBRIDGE

by Miss J. P. STRACHEY

Principal of Newnham College

WOMEN students who are working for the degree examinations of the University of Cambridge are required to belong to one of the two women's colleges, Girton or Newnham. Both these colleges were founded less than sixty years ago, and it is perhaps not one of the least interesting things about the higher education of women in Cambridge that it is of such recent growth. A general dissatisfaction with the state of girls' education in England began to make itself felt in the middle of the nineteenth century. The standard in boys' schools at that time was, if not high, at least higher than that in girls' schools because the schoolmasters had themselves been at the University, and it therefore seemed clear that the first step towards improving girls' schools must be to provide them with teachers who had had opportunities of getting a University education. But the early history of both Girton and Newnham shows how great were the difficulties which surrounded the question of helping women to get a University education, and how many were the doubts of those who looked on. What is now Girton College was started—largely by the efforts of Miss Emily Davies—in October 1869, in a house at Hitchin with five students; at first the lecturers came to Hitchin from Cambridge and from

London, but in 1873 the college was moved to its present site at Girton, about a mile and a half out of Cambridge on the Huntingdon Road. The beginnings of Newnham were equally inconspicuous. Mr (afterwards Professor) Henry Sidgwick and some of his friends had started lectures for women in Cambridge in 1869, and in 1871 he opened a small house at No. 74 Regent Street for five women students, who lived there under the care of Miss A. J. Clough. In 1875 Mr Sidgwick's venture moved into the oldest part of the buildings which are now Newnham College. They stand in grounds which lie to the west of Silver Street bridge and are about a quarter of an hour's walk from the middle of the town. Gradually, thanks to the energy, the devotion, and the prudence of the first founders, and thanks too to the zeal and hard work of the first students, what had been begun as an experiment proved itself to be a success. Every year the numbers of women who wanted to come to Cambridge increased: one new block of buildings after another sprang up at Girton and at Newnham until at the present time Girton comprises rooms for fourteen members of the staff and research Fellows and 189 students and research students, while Newnham contains 230 students (exclusive of a certain number of out-students) and rooms for 20 members of the staff and research Fellows. The grounds at Girton cover more than 45 acres and the buildings include a Dining Hall, a Library, a Chemical Laboratory, a Chapel, Lecture Rooms, and a Swimming Bath. Newnham stands in about 14 acres of gardens and playing fields; it too has a College Hall, a Library and Lecture Rooms.

Time has shown that the demand for University education for women was a real one and also that when it was offered them they could make good use of it. At first the women's lectures were carried on separately from those of the undergraduates; the

GIRTON COLLEGE

women students were examined only by the goodwill of the examiners and their place in the class lists was only made known privately. But by degrees Professors and lecturers began to admit women to University and college lectures, and in 1881 the University opened the Tripos (Honours) examinations to women, and required them to fulfil exactly the same conditions as to residence and examination as men students. A Statute passed in 1921 has enabled the University to grant titles of degrees to duly qualified members of the women's colleges. The number of women students is limited to five hundred. Under the new Statutes which came into force in 1926 the lecturers on the staffs of Girton and Newnham are admitted to take part in the educational work of the University. They may lecture and examine and may be members of Faculties and Faculty Boards. A large number of University prizes and scholarships have also been thrown open to women students.

The life of a woman student at Girton or Newnham is an active and busy one. Before she is admitted to college she has to pass the Previous Examination (or an examination exempting from it) and also either the Scholarship or the Entrance examination of the college. There are so many more candidates than vacancies that the competition is severe, and as the University admits women only to the Honours examinations a fairly high standard of knowledge is required. When she is safely in, she finds her time very fully taken up. Each college has a staff of lecturers and directors of studies in each of the different Tripos subjects, and one of these arranges the student's work with her and is ready to be appealed to if difficulties arise. The student attends lectures or laboratories in the University and classes and coaching in college. She may read in the University Library or in one of the Departmental Libraries or in her own College Library; but she probably prefers to take her books to her own room and work there in peaceful solitude. Meals are taken in common in the women's colleges—at Girton in the College Hall, at Newnham, where the students are divided into four halls of residence (Old Hall, Sidgwick

Hall, Clough Hall, Peile Hall), in the Dining Room of each Hall. In the afternoon most students play games—hockey, lacrosse, tennis, net-ball, fives, and the river attracts many, especially in the summer. The women are members of countless college and University societies, which meet once

NEWNHAM COLLEGE

a week or once a fortnight, mostly in the evenings; they attend concerts, theatres, and an occasional dance. Alongside of these activities is the business of making friends and of discussing everything in heaven and earth, though in this the woman student does not differ from the man student. And in the women's colleges, as in the men's, one of the charms of University life is the opportunity for meeting people of many different sorts.

The women's colleges are filled mainly of course

from the high schools and municipal and county secondary schools, but a number of students come from boarding schools, both the larger ones, such as Roedean or St Leonards, and the smaller private boarding schools. Now and then come girls who have been educated entirely at home, or who for special reasons have put off coming to college till they are older than the ordinary student. A certain number of students from overseas and from America are admitted every year. Some of these have graduated in their own Universities and are admitted to do post-graduate or research work; others read for the Tripos like the English girls.

It may be asked, "But what becomes of the Cambridge women after they leave the University?" The largest proportion of them is to be found in the secondary schools as assistant mistresses and head mistresses; there are also lecturers in Training Colleges and Universities, doctors, lawyers, social workers, civil servants, research workers, business women, journalists, writers, poor law guardians, members of local authorities, missionaries, magistrates, gardeners, farmers, librarians, secretaries, inspectors of factories, schools, trade-boards, health insurance, taxes. There is a member of Parliament and a member of two Statutory Commissions; and there are wives and mothers all over England and all over the world. Thus we may hope that the women students of Cambridge are trying to pay back, as far as in them lies, some part of the great debt they owe to the University.

THE DIARY
OF AN UNDERGRADUATE

by the Editor of *The Granta*

It is so easy to talk about "Cambridge" and "the 'Varsity" and to picture a herd of soulless and begowned undergraduates wholly obsessed with a passion for work, May-week and rags, and an intense rivalry with Oxford. That is the only conception that many parents possess of the place where they are sending their sons and daughters —"just for a 'Varsity education, you know, *so* good for them and *so* useful socially". And it comes as rather a shock to them to learn that the work done at Cambridge is—well, not as much as they thought, that barely fifty per cent. of the undergraduates stay up for May-week, that there are extraordinarily few rags and the greater part of the University seldom know anything about them until they see the next day's papers, and as for Oxford—well, the Boat Race and the Rugger match are largely an excuse for a jolly night in town, and Oxford and Cambridge are really so much of a unity that they are collectively referred to all over the country as "The 'Varsity".

Which is all very shattering, but not very constructive. What *does* Cambridge do during the six months of the year when it is in academic residence? And the answer is that there are some five thousand undergraduates, that they are all busy doing five thousand different things, and that they are all out to amuse themselves, which is the only characteristic they have in common.

This does not imply that they all spend their days and nights in dances and idleness and cocktail parties. If a man likes dances he will dance, and if he likes cocktails he will drink cocktails. But if he likes Beethoven he will play Beethoven, if he is fond of smells he will linger in the labs., and if he likes Sitwell he will read Sitwell. Each one to his taste, as they say in France. Probably they say it in several other countries as well: it is an excellent motto.

There are one or two regulations which every undergraduate must in his own interest observe. He must be in college or his rooms by midnight, wear cap and gown after dark, grumble at his Hall dinner, pass an exam. once a year, and tip the porters. He is also confronted with the alternative of attending a few lectures or persuading his Tutor that they are useless to him. For the rest he is a free agent.

Let us then pick a few specimens, and because Brown is the most conscientious of the lot and most nearly behaving as all fond parents imagine their sons are behaving at the 'Varsity, let us start with Brown.

"Call me daily at 7.30", says Brown to his bedder at the beginning of the term, "and breakfast at 8." And at 7.30 every morning of his life Brown leaps out of bed and at 8 o'clock he sits down to his boiled egg. Therein he differs from Smith, who is also called at 7.30 but who gets up at 8.30, while Robinson leaves a note every night to order his hot water at an hour in direct proportion to the hour at which he has gone to bed.

Walker, on the other hand—poor old Walker—
is not woken. "Leave me", he says, "till sleep
has fallen from me. I hate being woken up, it's
so bad for the nerves."

Nine o'clock finds Brown pedalling his way along
"K.P." or Trinity Street with a gown over his
shoulder and a pile of books under his arm. From
nine till one he is occupied with lectures, the
arguments of which he assiduously copies down
in his carefully-indexed notebooks. Then, having
slipped his glasses into their case and divested himself of his gown, he returns to his rooms (or some-
body else's rooms) to partake of lunch.

Thenceforth he is at liberty. Perhaps he will
spend the afternoon in some form of exercise,
perhaps he will go and watch the 'Varsity play
Rugger or take a walk to Grantchester. Perhaps,
on the other hand, he will sit down at his table and
work, for he is obviously an industrious fellow.
He will probably have tea with a friend, for tea is
essentially a social meal or nothing at all, and if
he has any time between then and Hall, he will
do "a spot more work".

At 6.30 or 7 o'clock or 7.30, or whatever time
it is, according to his year and college, he will
appear in Hall and eat dinner. And from then
until bed-time he may go to a cinema or a theatre
or a billiard saloon or a bridge party or any other
scene of public or private entertainment. Being
Brown, he will probably retire to his room and
work. And if he doesn't get a "First" at the end
of the year, at any rate he has the satisfaction of
knowing that he will go to heaven.

But what meanwhile of Jones, Smith, Robinson,
and Walker—poor old Walker? They are all

drifting along to their own caprice, for did not Disraeli once say that a University should be a place of learning, liberty, and light? Perhaps Jones has been to a couple of lectures or a supervision, and perhaps he hasn't. Smith—"exam.-next - month - you - know - must - do - something - about- it "—has settled down to do a little work. Robinson has met a few friends for coffee or has been buying a few things at a few shops. But he must hurry, for he is having an early lunch so as to be able to get to the golf course before the rush.

In the afternoon, while Robinson golfs and Brown works, Smith has a game of Rugger and Jones is down to row. Rowing is a sport happily designed for the benefit of those beings who are cursed with a self-torment complex. In Paris they have themselves crucified. But they all love it, and everyone loves to see them do it, so what need of pity? At any rate Jones is happy.

From four o'clock until dinner-time is rather an empty period, especially in the winter. Brown, of course, is doing a little work, and possibly Smith and Jones will do the same. But more likely they will have tea somewhere and talk and smoke the time away. Somehow there is always plenty to talk about.

But at night Cambridge wakes up and gets going, for distractions are plentiful. There are, to start with, some six or seven cinemas which are packed every night. There is the New Theatre, where the best of provincial companies come, and the Festival, where a gentleman called Mr Terence Gray provides a new brow-lifter every week; and there may be an undergraduate performance on at the A.D.C. or the Footlights. Brown, of course, is busy with his books, but Smith may be at the Union (if it is a Tuesday), at the Liberal Club (if it is a Thursday), or at the Conservative Association or the Labour Club (if it happens to be a Friday). Robinson is probably playing bridge— or possibly poker or *vingt-et-un*. Jones has got an old school dinner on, or a meeting of his college debating society or a musical club, or perhaps he has gone to a meeting of the League of Nations Union. And so the evening slips by and everyone is thoroughly contented and heedless of the future.

And Walker—poor old Walker—what of him? Walker is busy in his room, burning the midnight oil, scratching his head, and doing his best to write "The Diary of an Undergraduate", which he has promised for the National Union of Teachers.

THE TOWN OF CAMBRIDGE

by Brian W. Downs, M.A.

Fellow of Christ's College

Grantchester should be the name of this place and not of the little village made famous by Rupert Brooke's poem. As Grantacaestir it first appears in the *Ecclesiastical History of the English Nation* by the Venerable Bede; and as Kair-Grant, the Celtic equivalent, it was known to Henry of Huntingdon in the twelfth century and is known to the Welsh even at the present day. The present Grantchester owes its name to learned meddlers; in 1428 it was called Graunsete, which would have normally developed into Granset or Grantset.

The extraordinarily extensive and scattered urban entity now known as Cambridge comprises at least five distinct *nuclei*: coming down the river, first Newnham; then a settlement on the south side of Market Hill; after that, another settlement on the opposite bank near and beyond Magdalene College; fourth, Barnwell; and fifth, a little further down the river on the opposite bank, Chesterton. It is clear that the elements *caestir* and *Kair* in Grantacaestir and Kair-Grant indicate Roman origin. Two Roman roads passed through the present town: first, the so-called Via Devana, an important highway from Colchester (Camulo-dunum) to Godmanchester, where it joined the old North Road between London and Lincoln; and, second, a less important road coming in from the south-west and ultimately leading to Brancaster on the Norfolk coast. This last-named track kept to the west and north of the Cambridge river, and the intersection of these two roads occurred accordingly in or near the third of the five settlements just named, probably where the Histon Road now leaves the Huntingdon Road. Roman Cambridge therefore was essentially a "left-bank town". Traces of a Roman camp can still be seen in Mount Pleasant, a hundred yards or so from the intersection of the roads just described, and remains from a Roman cemetery have been discovered, not far off, in the garden of Magdalene College.

The next reference to the town after Bede's occurs in the Anglo-Saxon Chronicle, under date 875. By now it has changed its name and become Grantan Brycge, the Bridge in question standing on, or adjacent to, the site of the "Great Bridge" at Magdalene College. Applied to a settlement, however, it is doubtful whether at that time it denoted that to the north-west of the bridge, which seems to have remained the more important for another two or three hundred years, or to the southern settlement, expanding from the neighbourhood of Market Hill and destined ultimately to overshadow the other. However, an amalgamation between the two must soon have taken place, assisted no doubt by the establishment of a Danish colony round St Clement's Church, and later perhaps by the Jewry established in the reign of William the Conqueror on the north side of Market Street.

This dual town possessed considerable strategic and commercial importance. It was the lowest point on the river which could be crossed in the regular course of things, and therefore the natural road from the whole of East Anglia to the north of England passed through it. It seems too that the river was navigable to boats of fair draught. A considerable trade probably took place between the hithes on either side of the Bridge and King's Lynn, or even further. It must be borne in mind that the stone used later, for instance in the building of King's Chapel, came to Cambridge by water, and that within living memory much college wine was shipped in barges from King's Lynn.

With the draining of the Fens and the thinning of the forests to the south and east of Cambridge the corridor from East Anglia was widened and the importance of Cambridge declined. But in early Norman times it still figured fairly prominently in the annals of the country. William the Conqueror used it as a base for his operations against Hereward the Wake. The earliest architectural monument of the town, the tower of St Bene't's Church, dates from his time; and it was he who built, near the old Roman camp, a castle, the last portion of which disappeared in 1842.

But the sovereign with whom Cambridge seems to have had the closest connexion was King John. In 1207 he gave the town its first charter, with the valuable right of electing its own Provost or Mayor. During the reign of John, too, we hear not only of the first migration of scholars to the town and of the establishment of Stourbridge Fair (with both of which Mr Gaskoin and Miss Power have dealt elsewhere), but an attempt was made also to fortify the place. King John did not propose to turn it into a walled town; he confined himself to drawing a ditch round the half of the

ST BENE'T'S CHURCH

town lying further from the castle, which had by now become the more important. This King's Ditch started at the bottom of Mill Lane, crossed Trumpington Street just south of St Botolph's Church and the other main road at the Post Office, finally running into the river again on the west side of Midsummer Common. It had no military significance and seems to have been little else than a nuisance to the town. To its pestilential qualities, however, Cambridge is indebted for one of its most charming features, the little brooks that run down each side of Trumpington and St Andrew's Streets. They are part of "Hobson's Conduit", which was dug early in the seventeenth century mainly in order to scour the old ditch.

After King John's time Cambridge town, to the historian's eye, lapses into a kind of torpor. Lady Jane Grey was proclaimed Queen in the Market Place in 1553. Cromwell, who entered Parliament as member for the Borough, made Cambridge the centre of the seven Associated Protestant Counties; he placed a large gun on the bridge near Magdalene College and turned the old front court of St John's College into a prison for captured Royalists. Otherwise there is not very much to report of the history of the town apart from what may be recorded more appropriately in other chapters of this book. Newnham, Barnwell, and Chesterton grew towards the expanding centre and eventually became part and parcel of it, to form, at the last census, a town of about 60,000 souls. The name changed from Grantan Brycge to Cambridge and the river received the alternative appellation of Cam to the older Granta.

The chief monuments of past ages in Cambridge,

the town as distinguished from the University, are of course ecclesiastical. One of the earliest and most interesting of them, however, falls outside this category. It is the so-called "School of Pythagoras", the oldest monument in Cambridge north-west of the river, standing in private grounds to the south of Northampton Street and not very far from the fourth court of St John's College— as the crow flies. This is a very complete Norman dwelling-house: it has two storeys, the upper of which was the hall; the date assigned to it is 1150 to 1200, and it was probably the residence of some magnate, perhaps an official at the castle hard by. Why it is called the "School of Pythagoras" is a mystery. It certainly has nothing to do with the Greek philosopher, nor does it seem to have served an educational purpose at any time.

To the neighbourhood of the castle and the "School of Pythagoras" came the first Regulars, the Augustinian Canons who in 1112 moved to their final abiding-place at Barnwell. Barnwell Priory was a large and important house; but very little of it remains to-day. The curious, however, may explore an ancient wall and one building in Beche Road, commonly stated to have been the office occupied by the cellarer. The thirteenth-century parish Church of St Andrew's the Less on Newmarket Road, generally known as the Abbey Church, was not part of the Priory; but it was built by the Canons and served by them.

Many other Orders came to Cambridge in the wake of the Augustinians. The most interesting of their Houses was the Nunnery of St Radegund, mentioned in 1133 as "lately instituted", on its present site, which is that of Jesus College. In

1496 this institution, fallen into immorality and decay, was wound up and the buildings converted to their present use. The cloister court of Jesus, almost all of which dates from pre-collegiate times, is well worth a visit for its monastic features as well as for its architectural charms.

After this, nothing remains to be discussed here beyond the town churches. Of these, as has already been said, St Bene't's, or at any rate a portion of it, is the oldest. The tower is Saxon work, as the "long and short work" of the quoins shows. The nave dates from the late thirteenth century and details of the chancel from the fourteenth: otherwise the fabric is fairly new.

Two other interesting old churches lie almost equidistant from St Bene't's: the Church of King Edward the Martyr (who set up a mint in the town) to the north was and is a celebrated preaching church; to the south of St Bene't's, on the other side of Corpus Christi, lies the Church of the Fenland saint who favoured travellers, St Botolph. St Botolph's Church and Little St Mary's, about two hundred yards further along Trumpington Street, repay a visit, as Baedeker would say. St Botolph's, built about 1320, is most interesting for its little south chapel, raised a few inches above the level of the rest. It has, too, a font, the cover and case of which, dating from the reign of Charles I, are unique. Little St Mary's is a place of particular interest to all Americans, as it contains the tomb and funeral monument of an early Washington, who was Fellow of Peterhouse and whose arms display the crest and badge which the United States of America took over from another Washington of the same family.

St Michael's, opposite Caius, has an unusual central collegiate choir; St Andrew's the Great,

INTERIOR OF "THE ROUND CHURCH"

opposite Christ's, has a tablet to the memory of Captain Cook and his family; Christ Church, on the hither confines of Barnwell, is a monstrous perversion of King's College Chapel; Great St Mary's possesses some strange features, since it is partly a University Church and partly a parish Church; St Clement's is old and ugly. But the only two churches of note that remain to be discussed are the Round Church and the Leper's Chapel.

The Round Church, officially known as the Church of the Holy Sepulchre and St Andrew, situated at the junction of the two principal thoroughfares, was built in the first half of the twelfth century. There are only three other churches in this country distinguished by a circular nave. As the most celebrated of these is the Temple Church in London, it is generally assumed that this peculiarity is due to some connexion with the Order of Templars. But it is certain that this Cambridge Church never had any such connexion. The Lepers' Chapel, or Stourbridge Chapel, is a small flint edifice on the north side of the Newmarket Road just after it has crossed the main line from Cambridge to Ely. It dates from about the same time as the Round Church, but, whereas the Round Church has been barbarously "restored", the little chapel at Stourbridge still remains an essentially twelfth-century building, except for an alteration to the east window and a roof put in during the fifteenth century. It now belongs to the University and was put into an excellent state of repair by Sir Gilbert Scott in 1867.

CAMBRIDGE ARCHITECTURE

by THEODORE FYFE, M.A.

Director of the University School of Architecture

In thinking of Cambridge architecture, one in-
evitably compares it with that of Oxford, or
rather, one compares Oxford as a whole with
Cambridge. There is much that is instructive in
such a comparison, especially if it leads to the
conclusion that each should be accepted as a great
thing, independent of the other. A few words of
comparative analysis, however, may not be out of
place. Oxford is primarily a city of one great
street, with a lovely and fascinating by-way
parallel to it, a great cross-cut on the main street,
clusters of colleges and gardens round these, and
the dominating features of a fine dome and some
beautiful towers and spires. All of this is in a
valley and can be seen most admirably from heights
on the south and west. Cambridge is an East
Anglian market town in a flat country. There is
little that dominates from a distance except the
great bulk of King's College Chapel—with its four
immense turrets—and one fine modern spire.[1] The
river, before penetrating with its many fascinating
bridges the heart of collegiate Cambridge, strays
through fen lands and cuts across grassy banks
bridged many times. Quite a considerable, and
now increasing, part of the town and its college

[1] That of the Roman Catholic Church at the corner of
Lensfield Road and Hills Road, a good building by Messrs
Dunn of Newcastle, built in 1890.

buildings lies on the "other side" of the river: this is quite in contrast to Oxford.

Turning now to street architecture and to viewpoints generally, if there is nothing quite so thrilling as the centre of the High Street at Oxford leading to the sparkle of the great river at Magdalen tower, Cambridge has some memorable views and approaches. In this aspect, much depends on the time of the year and the time of the day. On the whole, Cambridge is never more fascinating than in spring and early summer, before the heavy foliage obscures so much that is of interest. On a great part of its western side, views of the colleges are controlled by regiments of trees. But walk up Trumpington Street, towards King's Parade, about midday on a bright sunny day and mark the deep broad shadow on the street, with King's turrets as the culmination of the view; or mark, with relief, the long, cool line of the front of Emmanuel and its pillared entrance after the somewhat drab walk or drive from the station to the town; or traverse the Backs road and proceed eastwards through St John's College grounds, when, early in the afternoon, you will be rewarded by the complete stretch of the college buildings rising, fairylike, through a mist of trees. These are only three notable views, and there are many others that make Cambridge a world of its own.

Cambridge has much to show in historic architectural achievement that is comparable to the glories of the sister University. At St Bene't's Church there is a Saxon tower including, inside, one of the finest Saxon arched openings in existence. The round Norman Church of St Sepulchre, though much restored, is still the substantial relic of one of the only four churches of the kind in England. The chancel of the Chapel of Jesus College is, for its size, as perfect an example of Early English building as can be seen anywhere. The greater part of the Church of St Mary the Less is an equally fine example of later Decorated

KING'S COLLEGE CHAPEL, FROM THE SOUTH

Gothic. Outstanding as these smaller examples are, they are excelled in general interest by two later buildings. The first of these, in point of date, is King's College Chapel, which might with truth be acclaimed as the glory of Cambridge, the most complete example of English Perpendicular Gothic in England and the greatest chapel in the world. The second is Sir Christopher Wren's Library at Trinity College, certainly one of the very greatest works of the great master of English architecture.

Cambridge, then, is rich in examples of positive historic architecture; and many more buildings and groups of buildings that are of absorbing interest can be added to this first list—the Old Court of Corpus Christi College; the Court of St Catharine's College; Great Court and Nevile's Court at Trinity College; the Gateway of St John's

SENATE HOUSE AND UNIVERSITY LIBRARY

College; Wren's Chapel (his first building) at Pembroke College—perhaps the finest Renaissance chapel in Oxford or Cambridge; the Court of Emmanuel College with Wren's Chapel as a centrepiece; Clare College from the garden of King's College; the Fellows' Building at King's College; the Cloister Court of Queens' College; the group of buildings formed by the Senate House and the University Library; and the Fitzwilliam Museum. One could go on adding to the list, but the intention is rather to indicate some things that should on no account be missed and which will amply repay careful study.

Nowhere better than in collegiate Cambridge, except at Oxford, can the contrast of Classic and Gothic methods of building be studied. A great Swedish architect—Ragnar Östberg, who visited this country last year—has recorded his impressions of Oxford (and particularly Christ Church) in words which include the following: "What an artistic domination lies embedded in these college gardens!.. The century-long battle between Classic peace and Gothic movement fuses here in a resplendent unity which has no parallel in European architecture". These are thoughtful words which are equally true of Cambridge. Herein lies the educative value of this architecture. No factor could be more decisive for good in the education of the young architect than the continued absorption of this "sense of unity".[1] To get full value from the quotation one has to realise what Classic peace and Gothic movement really mean, architecturally. This can be explained best by actual examples. Walking north up Trumpington Street one sees the insistent vertical lines of the eastern end of King's College Chapel, and beyond it the horizontal lines of the Senate House gradually

[1] The University School of Architecture, now on an assured basis, was started some years before the War with this conviction in view. It enables matriculated students of the University to obtain the ordinary B.A. Degree in Architectural Studies by a three years' course at once in conformity with the academic traditions of the University and of a thoroughly practical kind. Three of its students in the past two years have obtained important Scholarships at American Universities, while several others are now doing very good work in architectural practice.

unfolding—one of the finest street views in the world. As one proceeds, the long side of the Chapel is seen to consist of serried ranks of deeply projecting buttresses dividing immense storeyed windows terminating in the curved pointed arches of the Gothic builders. The Senate House also contains vertical lines in its columns and pilasters, but all is ordered and stationary. The vertical lines are severely controlled by the horizontal lines of the entablature at the top and the plinth or base at the bottom. This is the Classic principle and is universal in all buildings of complete Renaissance type. Gothic buildings might be defined as based on curvilinear forms and Classic buildings as based on rectilinear forms, the former being dependent on the arch and the latter on the beam. When once these general principles are understood, they can explain much that is obscure in the processes that occurred during the fusion of the two methods of building—a fusion that took place in this country from the reign of Henry VIII till the accession of Charles II—in other words from about the beginning of the sixteenth century till the middle of the seventeenth century. Cambridge is fruitful of examples showing the transition. A most conspicuous example (which ought to be bizarre, yet takes its place quite quietly) is the east end of Peterhouse Chapel, on Trumpington Street, where a traceried Gothic window is found associated with rudimentary pediment and mouldings of Classic form. Other examples can be seen in the Fellows' Building at Christ's College, the south front of Clare College, the oldest building of Emmanuel College, and the Heacham Building (south side, inner court) at Pembroke College, in

all of which the mullioned windows are Gothic in
character, though the general lines of the treat-
ment are Classic in greater or less degree.

Here, at the risk of being a little technical, it
is as well to emphasise another essential principle
that underlies all intelligent appreciation of historic architecture—the very ordinary one of
fenestration. The Gothic window was the product
of a structural expedient that governed the roofing
over of all the important church buildings of
medieval times with pointed vaults of stone.
Small windows, of course, were pointed, even
though not directly associated with vault construction, because this was the natural form for
arches of the period. The earlier ones were often
grouped as lancets. This principle of *grouping* is
found right through medieval work and brought
in the use of "mullions"—the vertical dividing
bars in large windows—which enabled the glass to
be used in small pieces divided by lead-work.
Even in Tudor and Elizabethan times, when
windows became square-headed (for convenience)
in domestic work, the grouping with mullions continued. In late Gothic times (before Tudor) the
"transome", or horizontal bar, was introduced
for additional strength. These can be seen, elaborately treated, in King's College Chapel. The combined use of mullion and transome was important
as it led to domestic windows of convenient size,
but still with small leaded panes, divided into
four-lights, by means of one mullion and one
transome. Such windows can be seen in many
Tudor and Jacobean buildings at Cambridge, as,
for example, Clare College and the Fellows'
Building at Christ's College. This type of window,

in fact, continued right through the seventeenth century and was not entirely superseded till Georgian architecture commenced. Then the sash window, divided into larger panes of glass by wooden bars, was introduced. A most interesting early example of this, built in 1704, is the Master's Lodge at Peterhouse.

Cambridge is rich in brick-work, while Oxford is without it. The use of brick in England is, of course, founded on Roman precedent. Saxons and Normans used brick, largely Roman brick, and East Anglia has used it traditionally, here and there, ever since those early days. But its general use was practically abandoned until its re-introduction from the Low Countries early in the sixteenth century. There is very good brick-work in Queens' College, Cloister Court; St John's College, first and second courts; Pembroke College, second court; and St Catharine's College, which is almost entirely of brick with stone dressings.

Carved woodwork is mostly of Jacobean date (early seventeenth century) but at Queens' College there is a fine mid-fifteenth-century door in the "Screens" (passage between Hall and buttery) which is thoroughly Gothic. The Jacobean examples are many. There are few Cambridge colleges which cannot show them. The most perfect example is the Combination Room of St John's College, with its panelling, untouched plaster ceiling, and two rich chimney pieces. The screen and stalls in King's College Chapel are in a class apart—they are of Spanish origin—but the screen in the Hall of Trinity College is more English. The priceless possession of all these things is their vigorous hand-workmanship. Of later Renaissance carved woodwork perhaps the finest Cambridge example is in the Chapel of Christ's College. Apart from special fitments and as examples of whole apartments where wood-work predominates, the Libraries of Jesus College and Peterhouse should on no account be missed.

THE COMBINATION ROOM, ST JOHN'S COLLEGE

It is impossible to do justice to the whole of the historic architecture of Cambridge in such a brief review, and attention must be re-directed to the period of the introduction of the sash window. Later Georgian architecture is represented principally by James Essex, who was responsible for most of the respectable, if slightly dull, stone-work of plain character to be seen in the first courts of Christ's College and Trinity Hall and the south-west corner of Great Court, Trinity. Essex's best work was the street front of Emmanuel, which does not include the spiritless later north end in

THE FITZWILLIAM MUSEUM

Victorian Gothic. The very end of the Renaissance tradition, as represented by Essex, gave place, early in the nineteenth century, to the "Classic Revival". Cambridge has two fine examples of this, both by architects of real distinction—the whole of Downing College, by William Wilkins, and the Fitzwilliam Museum, by Bassevi and Cockerell. Wilkins, at a later stage, proceeded to revive a heavy style of Gothic and executed the street front and first court of Corpus Christi College, as well as the Screen and Gatehouse of King's College; but all his work is marked by a certain largeness of handling. Nearly as good for "revival" work are Rickman's new buildings for St John's College, on the west side of the river. One cannot say so much for the later efforts of Waterhouse at Caius and Pembroke Colleges, but Cambridge is fortunate in possessing works by two of the greatest of the Gothic revivalists—G. F. Bodley's building at King's College and G. G. Scott's stone additions to Pembroke College, fronting on Pembroke Street but seen best from the Fellows' Garden. The last-named architect also added, with fine taste, an eastern bay to Wren's Chapel at Pembroke. Of the work of Scott's better-known father, Sir Gilbert Scott, Cambridge possesses comparatively little, but the tower of his Chapel at St John's is not unsuccessful.

In reflecting on the work of modern architects at Cambridge, one must remember that it is peculiarly difficult to preserve the true collegiate spirit in the midst of the tremendously strong historic associations of Cambridge. There are successful solutions. J. J. Stevenson, in his new building at Christ's College, and Mr T. H. Lyon, in his new building at Peterhouse, have both succeeded. It is impossible to judge the full effects of Mr Kennedy's new buildings at King's College and Sir Giles Scott's new buildings for Clare College (across the Backs) until both are completed, but the latter show one unit completed and this is certainly a distinguished work. The re-modelling of the interior of Sidney Sussex College Chapel by Mr T. H. Lyon is a *tour de force* of modern craftsmanship, informed by careful and sound detail.

Leaving collegiate architecture, we should note Messrs Smith and Brewer's completely successful galleries in the new wing of the Fitzwilliam Museum. If the general effect of the new buildings in Downing Street is rather depressing, it must be borne in mind that a street of this width was never intended for buildings other than the low, pleasant, old-fashioned ones which still remain at its west end opposite Pembroke College.

Very little has been said about the town of Cambridge as apart from the University; but rightly, in great part, the two factors form an indivisible whole. The town, as history (and it has had an eventful history for a much longer period than the University), can be felt most strongly in Bridge Street and Castle Hill. A ramble in this direction will disclose many things of interest. There is Magdalene College with its delightful Pepysian Library and quaint little Hall; St Peter's Church with a splendid twelfth-century font; and the venerable associations of Castle Hill, from which a very fair view of Cambridge can be obtained. Market Hill, with its booths, gives a quality to Cambridge which is priceless and its western side is dominated finely by the tower of Great St Mary's Church. The Guildhall falls pleasantly into the scheme of the whole and no new building could ever take its place satisfactorily that did not maintain its quiet grey colour.

Much has been done in the placing of modern buildings that could have been done much better, and, as usual in England, eye-sores crop up in the town outside the more soundly informed spheres of University and collegiate control; but the growing public sense of fitness in these things may, it is to be expected, produce better results in the future. Both at Cambridge and at Oxford it is now realised that the historic treasures of their architecture must suffer unless wise forethought is given to the inevitable growth of their surroundings.

STOURBRIDGE FAIR

by Eileen Power, Lit.D.

For English people to-day the word "fair" calls up a picture of merry-go-rounds and switchbacks, with perhaps a freak or two and a few stalls of sweets and ginger-bread and crockery. It is hard indeed to remember that such shows are the last degenerate remnant of an institution which was for many centuries the most important medium of international trade in Europe. The English fairs in the Middle Ages never attained quite the same importance as the great fairs of Champagne and the Netherlands, where you might meet traders from every quarter of Europe and buy almost every known product of nature or of the ingenuity of man, in the thirteenth and fourteenth centuries. Nevertheless a number of English fairs had much more than a national reputation and chief among them, both for its size and importance and for the length of its life, was Stourbridge Fair. "Below Cambridge to the East", writes Camden in his *Britannia* (1607), "near the little river Sture, every year in the month of September, is held the most famous fair in all England, whether in respect to the resort of people or the quantity of goods." It has its place in English literature as well as in English history, for tradition states that it was Bunyan's model for Vanity Fair, "where are all such Merchandize sold, as Houses, Preferments, Titles, Countreys, Kingdoms, Lusts, Pleasures and Delights of all sorts", and a vivid description of it has been left by that incomparable observer,

Daniel Defoe, in his *Tour through Great Britain* (1724).

Stourbridge Fair[1] was founded in 1211, when King John granted the lepers of the Hospital of St Mary Magdalen at Stourbridge a fair in the close of the Hospital, on the Vigil and Feast of the Holy Cross; the right to hold a fair was always a valuable gift, for the owner was by it enabled to take fees from the stall-holders and tolls from the merchants who came to buy. We know little about the early days of the fair, but it obviously rose in importance with the rise of the University at Cambridge, and references to it are common from the fourteenth century onwards. People journeyed to it to buy or sell from all parts of the country, and the accounts of the priories of Burcester (Oxon.) and Maxtoke (Warwickshire) in the early fifteenth century show that the monks, although over a hundred miles away, were wont to send there for victuals, harness, wainscot boards from the Baltic countries, brought by Hansard merchants, silk from Italy for vestments, Spanish iron and fish. The fair was specially noted for the sale of cloth and fish, for (as an act of 1533 asserts) it was, together with the neighbouring fairs of St Ives and Ely, "the most notable faire within this realm for provysions of fysshe".

From very early times both the town and the University of Cambridge got important privileges within the fair, and after the end of the Middle

[1] An excellent series of articles entitled *A Record of Stourbridge Fair* was published anonymously in *The Cambridge Review* for May 14, 1926, and subsequent numbers. I am much indebted to it for most of the information in this account.

Ages, when the leper hospital had disappeared, they shared its control. The fair was set out annually on September 4 by the Mayor and Corporation in procession, with music playing before them; they rode round the boundaries and proclaimed the limits of the fair. It was held in some cornfields between the Cam and the Stour, and one of its main advantages was that heavy goods could thus approach it by river as well as by road. If by September 4 all the harvest on these fields had not been gathered in, the booth-holders could trample down the corn and set up their booths. On St Bartholomew's Day the fair was opened by the Mayor and Vice-Chancellor and it lasted until St Michael's Day, when all booths and merchandise had to be cleared away, or the farmers could knock them down and confiscate them. Like most other fairs, it was laid out in regular rows and streets, in which each trade had its appointed place, the Duddery for woollen goods, Cheapside for mercery and grocery, Soper Lane for goldsmiths, Pewtry Row and Brazier Row for tinsmiths, Garlick Row for booksellers, Fish Hill for the fish stalls, Joiners' Row and Turners' Row for carpentry. The Mayor of Cambridge and the Chancellor of the University each had his booth, where he feasted his friends, and there was a court-house where were held the fair courts, or courts of "pie powder" (*pied poudré*, dusty foot) as they were called, because the dusty-footed trader came hurrying to them with disputes about false measure or false dealing, debts or assault. There were also show booths and ale-houses and eating-houses and much merry-making as well as trade.

Many and bitter were the quarrels between the town and the University (always in those days on bad terms with each other) about their respective rights in the fair, and constant were their petitions and counter-petitions to Parliament and to the Privy Council, especially in Elizabeth's reign. At last, however, they came to an agreement about the terms of their respective charters in 1589. The town was empowered to make rules for the fair, for setting up and disposing of the booths and for placing the different merchants and tradesmen in the places assigned to them. The University was granted the right of holding the assize or assay of bread, wine, ale, or beer and the supervision of weights and measures, with all fines and forfeitures resulting therefrom; the right to inquire into and punish cases of forestalling, regrating, and engrossing, and the power to search for and punish common women, vagabonds, and other suspect persons. There were to be two proclamations of the fair, one by the Mayor and the other by the Vice-Chancellor, and they were to take it in turns to make the first proclamation in alternate years. Both were to hold courts in the fair; the inspection of all goods except leather and sack-cloth was to be made by four "indifferent, discreet, honest, wise and able men, two to be appointed by the town and two by the University"; the examination and search of leather and sack-cloth were to belong to the town, in return for an annual payment of 3s. 4d. to the University. All cases arising out of this inspection were to be tried in alternate years by the Chancellor and Mayor and all forfeitures were to be equally divided between the town and the University.

The fair continued to be of great importance as a place of trade all through the seventeenth and early eighteenth centuries. From time to time new commodities appear for sale—tobacco (date uncertain), bibles (mentioned 1591), woven stockings (1600), tea. We hear, too, of play-actors; in 1592 the University complained to the Privy Council that a company "of certaine lighte persons pretending themselves to be her Majestys plaiers" had infringed the University decree against the acting of plays within five miles of Cambridge by playing their interludes at Chesterton, near the fair, and had actually proclaimed them "by settinge up of writinges about our College gates", which "vain games", the University asserts, would "drive our students from their books". The University found no less difficulty in enforcing its decree in the eighteenth century. "The *Cambridge Chronicle*, which appeared weekly from the middle of the eighteenth century", says a writer in *The Cambridge Review*, "contained advertisements each year of companies of players from London, Norwich or Sadlers Wells, who ranked among the great attractions of the Fair. Gunning, writing towards the end of the century, says that there were generally two theatres, which always attracted crowded audiences. Members of the University habitually came up ten days or a fortnight before the beginning of term on purpose to attend the theatrical performances at the fair. *The Beggar's Opera* was performed at Sturbridge in 1767."

The most famous account of the fair in the eighteenth century is that of Defoe in 1724, to which reference has already been made and which shows that it was still a great centre of trade. We cannot do better than quote a part of this description. Speaking of the Duddery, Defoe says:

This Place is separated and Peculiar to the Whole-sale Dealers in the Woollen Manufacture. Here the Booths or Tents are of a vast Extent, have different Apartments and the Quantities of Goods they bring are so Great, that the Insides of them look like another Blackwell Hall, being as vast Ware-houses pil'd up with Goods to the Top. In this Duddery, as I have been inform'd, there have been sold One Hundred Thousand Pounds worth of Woollen Manufactures in less than a Week's time, besides the prodigious Trade carry'd on here, by Wholesale-Men, from London and all Parts of England, who transact their Business wholly in their Pocket-Books, and meeting their Chapmen from all Parts, make up their Accounts, receive Money chiefly in Bills and take Orders: These they say exceed by far the Sales of Goods actually brought to the Fair and deliver'd in Kind; it being frequent for the London Wholesale Men to carry back Orders from their Dealers for Ten Thousand Pounds worth of Goods a Man, and some much more....

Here are Clothiers from Hallifax, Leeds, Wakefield and Huthersfield in Yorkshire and from Rochdale, Bury &c. in Lancashire, with vast Quantities of Yorkshire Cloths, Kerseyes, Pennistons, Cottons &c. with all sorts of Manchester Ware, Fustians and things made of Cotton-Wool; of which the Quantity is so great that they told me there were near a Thousand Horse-Packs of such goods from that side of the Country, and these took up a side and a half of the Duddery at least....

But all this is still outdone, at least in show, by two Articles which are the peculiars of this Fair and do not begin till the other Part of the Fair, that is to say for the Woollen Manufacture, begins to draw to

a Close: These are the Wooll and the Hops, as for the
Hops, there is scarce any Price fix'd for Hops in
England, till they know how they sell at Sturbridge
Fair; the Quantity that appears in the Fair is indeed
prodigious, and they, as it were, possess a large part of
the Field on which the Fair is kept, to themselves....

The quantity of Wool only, which has been sold at
this place at one Fair, has been said to amount to
fifty or sixty Thousand Pounds in value, some say a
great deal more.

By these Articles a Stranger may make some guess
at the immense Trade carry'd on at this Place; what
prodigious Quantities of Goods are bought and sold here
and what a confluence of People are seen here from all
Parts of England....

To attend this Fair and the prodigious conflux of
People which come to it, there are sometimes no less
than fifty Hackney Coaches, which come from London
and ply Night and Morning to carry the People to and
from Cambridge; for there the Gross of the People
lodge; nay, which is still more strange, there are
Wherries brought from London on Waggons to plye
upon the little River Cam and to row People up and
down from the Town and from the Fair as Occasion
presents. It is not to be wondered at if the Town of
Cambridge cannot Receive or Entertain the Numbers
of People that come to this Fair; not Cambridge only,
but all the Towns round are full; nay, the very Barns
and Stables are turn'd into Inns and made as fit as
they can to Lodge the meaner Sort of People.

Gunning in the later years of the eighteenth
century gives an almost equally vivid account of
the fair as it was in his time, naming especially a
Mr Green of Limehouse who dealt in grocery and
pickles; his booth was three times as large as any
other in the fair and all the neighbouring families

laid in their stores from him, while the young gentlemen of the University went to gaze at his beautiful daughter, whom they called "Miss Gherkin". He made from £1500 to £2000 during the fair. A writer in *The Mirror* in 1828, giving his own recollections of the fair some fifty years before, mentions that his father used to bring home £1000 in cash, over and above his credit sales, and that Messrs Cox and Herne, silk mercers of Holborn, never had less than £2000 of goods in stock. Nevertheless the importance of the fair as a place of commerce was waning in the last part of the eighteenth century, and with the dawn of the nineteenth it had already become primarily a place of amusement. The Vice-Chancellor's Court was held for the last time in 1855, and though the Mayor of Cambridge still proclaims the fair every year, it has now dwindled to complete insignificance, even as a pleasure centre.

ELY CATHEDRAL

by The Very Rev. A. F. KIRKPATRICK
Dean of Ely

THE Cathedral Church of Ely owes its existence
to the faith and devotion of St Etheldreda, who
founded a monastery at Ely A.D. 673. She was
the daughter of Anna, King of the East Angles,
and was born at Exning near Newmarket. About
the year 652 she became the wife of Tonbert,
prince of the south Gyrvii, who gave her the Isle of
Ely as a marriage settlement. Three years afterwards he died, and Etheldreda retired to her home
at Ely. Three years later she was induced to leave
it to marry, doubtless for political reasons, Egfrid,
son of Oswy, King of Northumbria, who succeeded
his father in 670. But Etheldreda had no love for
the gaieties of the court and longed to devote
herself to a life of piety and devotion. In the year
673 she returned to Ely to found the monastery,
of which she was consecrated Abbess by her
friend Wilfrid, the Archbishop of York. She died
in 679.

Of the church and monastery which she built
nothing now remains. It was entirely destroyed
in the terrible invasion of 870, when East Anglia
was ruthlessly devastated by the Danes. But one
most precious link of connexion with the times and
the household of St Etheldreda still survives. In
the south aisle of the nave of the Cathedral may

be seen the base and part of the shaft of a cross
with the Latin inscription

LVCEM · TVAM · OVINO

DA · DEVS · ET · REQVIĒ

AMEN

"Thy light to Ovin grant, O God, and rest. Amen."

Ovin was Etheldreda's chief minister or steward
for the management of her estate. The cross,
originally erected to his memory at Haddenham,
was fortunately brought into the Cathedral in
the eighteenth century to preserve it.

During the century after the Danish invasion
the continuity of religious life and worship at Ely
was maintained by a body of secular clergy, until
in 970, under the auspices of King Edgar, Dunstan
the Archbishop of Canterbury, and Ethelwold
the Bishop of Winchester, a regular Benedictine
monastery was established. Dunstan and Ethelwold both took part in the consecration of the new
Church. From this time until the Dissolution of
the Monasteries in the reign of Henry VIII it was
the Church of a rich and important Benedictine
Monastery.

For the next century Ely had peace. Two in-
cidents in this period may be recalled. We are all
familiar with the quaint lines in which Canute is
said to have expressed his delight in the chanting
of the monks of Ely, which he often visited; and
Edward the Confessor is recorded to have spent
some time at Ely as a child, and learnt psalms and
hymns along with the boys in the cloister school.

At the Norman Conquest the Isle of Ely became
a Camp of Refuge, and the story of the heroic

stand made there against William by the Saxons
under Hereward is familiar to readers of Kingsley's
Hereward the Wake. It was not till 1071 that Abbot
Thurstan came to terms with William, and the
Isle was surrendered. We may picture the angry
Conqueror striding up the Church and flinging
a mark on the altar as his offering, and then imposing a fine of 700 marks on the monastery, which
he increased to 1000 marks when short weight
of the amount was brought to him at Cambridge.

But William did Ely an inestimable service
when he sent there as Abbot in 1081 Simeon the
Prior of Winchester, whose brother Walkelin was
Bishop of Winchester. This grand old man undertook to rebuild the entire monastery, and in 1083,
when he was 90 years old, laid the foundation of
a new Church, planned on a magnificent scale.
The simple Norman arches in the ground-story of
the eastern transepts are probably his work. He
lived to the age of 100, but could only see the
beginning of his bold design, though his plan
has left its stamp on the structure of the whole
Cathedral. It was not till 1106 that the Church,
though still far from completion, was sufficiently
advanced to be dedicated, and on October 17 of
that year the bodies of St Etheldreda and her
fellow-saints were removed into it with great
pomp and ceremony.

Three years afterwards (1109) the Bishopric of
Ely was constituted, and the Church while still
remaining a monastic Church, became a Cathedral
Church, i.e. a Church in which a bishop has his
cathedra or official seat. The Bishop took the place
of the Abbot at Ely, and the internal government
of the monastery was in the hands of the Prior.

ELY CATHEDRAL FROM THE OUSE

Hence arose the peculiarity at Ely that the Bishop does not, as is usually the case, occupy a "throne" to the east of the choir stalls, but sits in the return stall at the west end of the choir on the south side; while the Dean, as the successor of the Prior, occupies the corresponding stall on the north side.

After 1106 the building of the nave proceeded slowly, probably with interruptions. Happily the same simple type of Norman architecture was preserved throughout, with comparatively slight variations. But by the time that the Western Tower and transepts were being built architectural style was beginning to change. The original tower arches, which are to be seen above the solid arches built under them some two centuries later to make the tower safe, are pointed, though they have mouldings of Norman character. The south transept is a fine example of the more elaborate late Norman work. The interlacing arcades on the west wall are an effective form of decoration. Bp. Geoffrey Riddell (1174–89) is recorded to have finished the new work towards the west and carried the tower almost to its summit. The top story of the present tower is of course a much later addition, towards the end of the fourteenth century. It is not certain that the north transept, now missing, was ever actually completed, though no doubt some part of it must have been built to buttress the tower. There is no record of its fall or destruction.

The two doorways on the south side of the nave, commonly called the Prior's Door and the Monks' Door, are fine examples of late Norman sculpture.

Thus by A.D. 1200 the Norman Church was complete. Three points must be remembered in regard to it. Eastwards it extended only one bay

beyond the present choir stalls. It had a square
central tower at the crossing of the nave and

PRIOR'S DOOR, ELY CATHEDRAL

transepts; and the monks' choir, where they held
their daily services, was separated from the rest
of the nave by a solid stone screen, standing just
to the west of the present Octagon.

The next addition was the Western Porch, called
The Galilee, built by Bishop Eustace (1198–1215).
It is an early and notable example of the Early
English style of architecture which prevailed during the first three quarters of the thirteenth century.
The origin of the term "Galilee" for a western porch,
or as at Durham, chapel, is uncertain. Some
think that it was so called on the analogy of the
Court of the Gentiles in the Temple (Galilee of the
Gentiles); others that the name originated from
a fanciful application of the text "He goeth before
you into Galilee" (Mk xvi. 7) to the priest who led
the great Sunday procession to the westernmost
part of the Church.

A generation later Bishop Hugh de Northwold
(1229–54) took down the Norman east end, and
lengthened the Cathedral by the six eastern bays,
known as the Presbytery. It was begun in 1235,
and dedicated on September 17, 1252, in the
presence of King Henry III and his son, afterwards
Edward I, and a great assembly of prelates and
nobles. Its design and proportion and the richness
of the carving make it one of the finest examples
of the Early English style to be seen in this country.
Later alterations, however, have detracted from the
beauty of the original design. The two western
bays of the triforium were replaced by late
fourteenth-century windows, and all the aisle
windows were similarly altered.

In 1322 a disaster befell the Cathedral, which
proved to be a fortunate disaster, inasmuch as it
resulted in the construction of the characteristic
feature of the Cathedral, the central Octagon.
The central Norman tower fell with a tremendous
crash, destroying the bays of the Norman choir

to the east. Happily the Sacrist of the monastery, Alan de Walsingham, was a man of supreme genius and indomitable courage. Instead of re-building a square tower, he opened out the centre of the Church into a spacious Octagon, over which he raised a beautiful Lantern, lighted by eight windows. It is a most ingenious construction of timber, covered externally with lead. Alan had to search far and wide for timber of sufficient size, especially for the great angle posts of the Lantern. At the same time the three bays to the east of the present choir screen, which had been ruined by the fall of the tower, were rebuilt at the expense of Bishop Hotham. All this work was carried out in the Decorated style of the period. The beautiful canopies of the choir stalls are of the same date; the groups of figures in them are modern: they were carved at Louvain in Belgium.

While all this work was going on, the famous Lady Chapel to the north of the choir was being built under the care of John of Wisbech, one of the monks. When it was in its perfection with its stained glass windows, brilliantly coloured walls, and wealth of statuary and tabernacle work, it must have been one of the most magnificent buildings in the country. But windows and statues were destroyed, and figures in the taber-nacle work decapitated, at the Reformation.

Important works were also being carried on in the domestic buildings of the monastery, and it is a problem how money and skilled artisans were found for the work done between 1321 and 1349, when all progress was brought to an end by the terrible visitation of the Black Death, which depopulated East Anglia.

Thus by 1349 the main fabric of the Cathedral was complete. It was the work of three centuries, and it combined into a remarkably harmonious unity three great styles of English architecture, Norman of the twelfth century, Early English of the thirteenth, and Decorated of the fourteenth. The proportions of the ground-story, the triforium, and the clerestory, fixed by Simeon and the Norman builders in the eleventh century, were adhered to by Hugh de Northwold when he extended the Cathedral in the thirteenth century, and by Alan de Walsingham when he rebuilt the three bays of the choir in the fourteenth century.

Two additions remain to be noticed. Bishop Alcock's Chapel (1488) at the east end of the north aisle of the choir is an extraordinarily elaborate specimen of late Perpendicular architecture: and Bishop West's Chapel (1534) at the east end of the south aisle of the choir is remarkable for its Renaissance ornamentation, executed probably by Italian craftsmen.

At the Reformation Henry VIII dissolved the monastery and replaced the Prior and monks by a Dean and Chapter of eight canons with a full cathedral establishment. But even in this radical change there was continuity; for the last Prior was appointed as the first Dean, and some of the monks were made canons. Some of the monastic buildings were pulled down as no longer needed; and the iconoclasm of the Reformers in the reign of Edward VI did irreparable mischief to the imagery of the Lady Chapel. During the Commonwealth the fabric of the Cathedral does not seem to have suffered seriously, though more of the monastic buildings were removed, or incorporated

ELY CATHEDRAL, TOWER FROM SOUTH SIDE

into houses; and the Cathedral Services were of course suspended.

In modern times a complete restoration has been carried out. It was begun by Dean Peacock in 1845, and was under the direction of Sir G. G. Scott. The nave roof was painted by Mr L'Estrange of Hunstanton and Mr Gambier Parry. The Reredos was given by Mr Dunn Gardner of Chatteris in memory of his wife. The War Memorial Chapel in the north transept records the names of 5400 men of Cambridgeshire and the Isle of Ely who gave their lives for their country in the Great War.

Space forbids more than a brief mention of the domestic buildings of the monastery. Such portions as remain have been for the most part incorporated in the Deanery and the canons' and other houses. The Cloister, which next to the Church was the centre of the daily life of the monastery, lay to the south of the nave. All that now remains of it is a part of the north alley converted into vestries and part of the east alley leading to the south-east door into the Cathedral. The Refectory was on the south side of it. The Chapter House, where the monks met daily for business, opened out of the eastern alley, but this, and also the Dormitory, have been entirely destroyed. To the south of the choir was the Infirmary with its Chapel, always an important part of a Benedictine monastery. The columns and arches with elaborate Norman mouldings, now built into the adjacent houses, show that it must have been a remarkably fine building, erected probably about 1160–70. The great Guest Hall, built in the thirteenth century and much altered in the fourteenth, was converted into a dwelling-house, probably during the Commonwealth, and is now the Deanery. The Norman columns and arches near its entrance are the remains of the monks' Kitchen. To the south of the Guest Hall was the Prior's Lodging, now a canon's house, and adjoining it is Prior Crauden's Chapel, a gem of fourteenth-century architecture (c. 1326). It is now used by the King's School. The lofty windows opposite belonged to the Queen's Hall, said to have been built by Prior Crauden for the entertainment of Edward III and Queen Philippa. Further on to the south is the noble gateway known as Ely Porta (c. 1400), which was the principal entrance to the monastery. Near this is the Great Barn, now utilised for the school gymnasium. To the west of the Cathedral stands the Bishop's Palace. The name of the road between them, "The Gallery", preserves the memory of the Gallery or Passage, long ago pulled down, which once connected the Palace with the Cathedral. The wings of the Palace were built by Bishop Alcock (1486–1501); the central part between them by Bishop Keene (1771–81); and the Long Gallery to the west by Bishop Goodrich (1534–54).

A little further west stands St Mary's Church, close to which is the house, now St Mary's Vicarage, which was Oliver Cromwell's home from 1636 till he removed to London in 1646.

THE CAMBRIDGESHIRE FENS AND THEIR DRAINAGE

by J. JONES

Lecturer in Geography, Homerton College

MOST countries have their areas of imperfect drainage, and to this England is no exception. Chief among such areas in England is the one called the Fens; and since about two-thirds of Cambridgeshire belongs to this tract of fenland, we have in this fact the reason for the inclusion of this article in the *Souvenir*.

The Fenland is, roughly, an oval area broken into in the north-east by an arm of the North Sea called the Wash, which in times past was much larger than at present and perhaps almost co-extensive with the Fenland. This oval area has its longer axis, about sixty miles, from north to south, the shorter one from east to west, thirty miles. The rivers Witham, Welland, Nene, and Great Ouse flow from the surrounding higher lands across the Fens to the Wash. The phrase "across the Fens", rather than "through the Fens", is used purposely, for the beds of the rivers are usually higher than the surrounding lands.

It is exactly fifty years since Messrs Miller and Skertchly published their standard work entitled *The Fenland, Past and Present*, a volume running to over six hundred pages, and even there the whole story is not told; so it is clear that in the space available it will only be possible to look at some few features of the Fenlands.

To anyone crossing the Fenland to-day there is plenty of evidence that here we have an area that has been subdued by man. Hundreds of straight drains of varying widths, stretching as far as the eye can follow them, intersect each other in a rectangular pattern over the surface of the land. Usually they are full of stagnant water, which has percolated in from the adjacent fields, and which, when the time comes, will be pumped into the rivers and so reach the sea. The rivers themselves also have an artificial appearance. To reach a river we have first of all to walk up a rather steep bank. Having reached the top of this bank, we descend into a dry bed, should the river not be in flood, and then climb a second bank at the bottom of which is the river. The same features probably occur on the other side also. Such a stream is said to be double-banked. The beds between the banks are called "washes" and are made to take the flood waters when the river overflows.

Flatness is the prevailing topographical characteristic of the Fens. As far as the eye can see in all directions the level land appears to meet the sky on the distant horizon. Yet that the surface is not perfectly level is a fact that the careful observer detects. Occasionally, and especially in the Cambridgeshire Fens, we find patches of land slightly higher than that which surrounds them. These eminences—low, it is true, but high enough to differentiate them from the encircling lands— are called "islands". They well deserve the name, for they have played the same important part in the settlement and development of the Fens as islands in a sea, or oases in a desert. The rains that fall, and the waters that are brought by streams and rivers, into the Fens have great difficulty in finding their way to the sea, for everywhere the gradients are so weak that the land becomes water-logged, and these islands form the drier spots, slightly better drained and hence more suitable for man's habitations.

And often between the "islands" are hollows, shallow, it is true, but deep enough for water to accumulate in them. These form the "meres".

We might then be able to form some idea of the Fens in their primeval state before man began his campaign against them—a campaign that began a couple of thousand years ago and is still going on.

Let us picture to ourselves an elliptical stretch of country of thirteen hundred square miles in area, a plain on which there rises not a single hill, over the surface of which is stretched in net-work fashion a maze of waterways, with frequent shallow expanses of water—the meres—and occasionally "islands" rising a few feet above the watery surface. But much of the water would be hidden from view by a characteristic vegetation of sedges and rushes which grew to a height of several feet. Probably along the more important rivers alders and willows would be seen, and on the drier "islands" broad-leaved trees such as the oak and elm would be found. Even to-day the vegetation on the "islands" differs considerably from that on the lower lands. Extensive views can be obtained, in which perhaps not a single tree interrupts the view; even hedges are absent, their places being taken by drains; but on the better drained "islands" large trees grow luxuriantly.

To those who know the Fens well the difference

between "island" and true fenland can be sensed by sight and scent, and the railway-traveller who may be a stranger to the region, if he puts the carriage window to good use, will have no difficulty in recognising the differences between the vegetation of "island" and fenland.

The Fens have played a characteristic rôle in the political and economic history of the land during the last two thousand years. While in their natural condition, they formed, first of all, a barrier to man's movements. If we have envisaged them aright, we must at once recognise their impassability. So if man wished to move from the lands to the east of the Fens into the midlands of the country, he had perforce to circumvent them, and this could only be done by journeying southwards. In the second place they were a defence, and thus people living in the land we now call Norfolk, having the sea as a defence on east and north, had the Fens, even a stronger defence, on the west, and thus could be attacked only from the south. Thirdly they were a refuge, either to the individual or to a band of men who knew the intricacies of their waterways. Woe to the pursuer if, ignorant of the Fens, he ventured to follow his enemy into that sea of reeds and rushes! All these phases of the influence of the Fens can be illustrated by many instances which are known to the student of our history. In the fourth place, the Fens were a store-house of food in the days when man lived by hunting and collecting the provisions afforded by nature. The waters abounded in fish, and numberless water-fowl made their habitation among the reeds; both fisher and fowler drew supplies from this waste of waters for themselves and their dependents. But what a change has taken place in these Fenlands since those far-off days! If the fowler of old could return, he would fail to recognise his old haunts. With much hard work the marshy wastes of ancient times have been reclaimed, but ceaseless vigilance against the ever-threatening waters is required in order to hold what has been gained. As I am writing this I take up a local newspaper, from which I extract the following as an illustration:

The Ouse Drainage Board—Meeting on Dec. 27th 1927: (1) It was reported that the banks of the Hundredfoot River between Welmore Lake Sluice and Denver Sluice were low and in an unstable condition, and a scheme, which will cost nearly £3500 and includes the purchase of a drag line excavator, is in contemplation. (2) The engineer had reported that the upper section of the river Nar above Wormegay High Bridge was getting into a thoroughly bad state, owing to the sinking of the banks and the silting of the bed of the stream. Suitable materials for making up the banks could be obtained at two points, but owing to the shoals the maximum load that could be boated amounted to about a ton. The cost of raising several miles of bank in this area was thought prohibitive. At present the margin between normal water-level and the level of the top of the banks in many places was small, with the result that with a small increase in the flow of the river the banks were overtopped with consequent flooding. The cost of dredging the two miles of the river Nar urgently requiring attention would be about £392.

But man's work and outlay have been repaid a thousand times over by the crops he garners every year from the fertile Fens; for to-day, by a close intensive agriculture, the Fenlands yield crops second to none throughout the British Isles.

The story of this reclamation has been told and retold in many ways. It is closely associated with the river system, and for the Cambridgeshire Fens the Great Ouse in its lower course must be studied. This river enters Cambridgeshire at Earith, after draining the clay lands of Bedford and Huntingdon, and later it is enlarged by several tributaries from the south and east. It carries towards the sea a large body of water, which is held up by the inflowing tide, and thus the danger of overflowing its banks was always possible until man undertook the work of harnessing the river to his needs. But even now the danger is ever present, and any point of weakness is at once seized upon by the enemy and thousands of acres may become flooded in a single night.

It will be hardly possible to give the story of the Great Ouse without reference to diagrams, and so the reader is asked to refer to those prepared for this purpose. In the diagram on page 90 we see the main river as it probably was, say a thousand years ago. It enters the county of Cambridge at Earith, and there divides into two branches, which unite again before reaching Wisbech. The one flows north-north-west, enters the Old Nene at Benwick, and thence to Wisbech. The other branch flows eastwards and then northwards round the Isle of Ely to Littleport. From here it follows a very meandering course north-westwards, joining the Old Nene to the south of Wisbech, and then past this old town to the Wash. Only a few of the tributaries are shown, but a reference to the diagram on page 93, which is

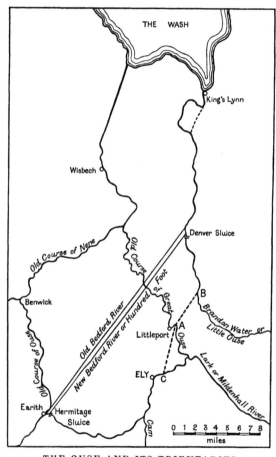

THE OUSE AND ITS TRIBUTARIES

copied from a map drawn in 1604 and is the earliest large scale map I have found, will indicate the intricate system of waterways between these two branches of the Ouse. Space does not permit to give all the evidence that this was the original course of the river; it must suffice to say that both geological and documentary evidence are available to establish the correctness of the diagram.

The diagram (p. 90) also shows, by a dotted line between *A* and *B*, the first great change in the drainage of which there is much traditional and other evidence. It will be seen that the Great Ouse was joined to the Little Ouse between Littleport and Brandon Creek, thus diverting a great volume of water from the former river into the latter, which discharges into the Wash at King's Lynn. It is not known exactly when and by whom this diversion was made, but it would appear that it was carried out before the time of the Conqueror. Apparently something like the following occurred. The bed of the river below Wisbech silted up, and the water repeatedly caused serious floods on the land to the north and north-west of Littleport. The people in this area, without consulting the authorities at King's Lynn, undertook the work of cutting the channel from the Great to the Little Ouse and thus brought about the great change. The following extracts from Dugdale's *History* refer to this:

So long as the outfall of Wisbeche had its perfect being, the whole river of Ouse had there its perfect outfall, from whence the town seemeth to have taken its denomination viz. *Ouse or Wisbeche*....Then, as it seemeth there was no river between Littleport and Brandon Water....But Wisbeche outfall decaying, and the passage of Nene by Crowland likewise failing,

the first branch of Ouse with Nene united waxed weak
in the passage and the most part thereof turned back
again to Littleport. This second branch of Ouse being
thereby debarred a passage by Wisbeche means were
made to let it fall from Littleport to Brandon Creek
by a lode which in the first seemed to be called
Hemming's Ea.... But the people of Marshland,
finding themselves overcharged by these waters, upon
complaint made to King Edward the First obtained
a commission, an. 21. Edw. I (A.D. 1294) to have the
waters (which anciently had their outfall by Wisbeche)
to be brought and carried into their ancient course.

The diagram also shows the important waterways at the present time. The principal change has
been the construction of the two Bedford rivers
or canals. These were built in the first half of the
seventeenth century, as part of the scheme of the
Dutchman Vermuyden, who was employed by
the Duke of Bedford to drain the southern Fens.
The object of these artificial rivers was to divert
the Ouse water, where it entered the Fens, into a
more direct path to the sea. To accomplish this,
great sluice-gates had to be built across the river
at Earith, called the Hermitage Sluice, and also
at Denver. The first of these diverted the water
into the canals, and the latter functioned in two
ways, for it prevented the canal water from running up the Ouse towards Littleport and it
diverted the tides into the canals. This extensive
scheme has been severely and adversely criticised
by many, but it is still working. Quite recently
new sluice-gates at Denver, costing several thousand pounds, have been built. It is pretty clear
that the Denver Sluice, by holding back the water
in the river, would cause it to deposit in its bed silt

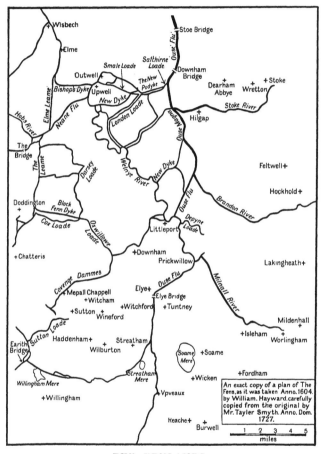

THE FENLANDS

which previously had found its way to the sea, so that between Denver and Ely conditions were worse than before. However, space forbids criticism, and the only thing we can do here is to state facts. The diagram also shows that the river has been straightened between Ely and Littleport, indicated by the dotted line C to A. This cut was opened exactly a hundred years ago and the river no longer flows by the circuitous path, but the old banks and bed can of course still be seen.

The diagram on page 93, as already mentioned, is a copy of an old map. The original is in the Cambridge Borough Library, and by the courtesy of the Librarian I was allowed to make the tracing. If compared with the other diagram, which only shows main water lines, it should help us to form some idea of this part of the Fens at the time of the cutting of the Bedford rivers. It will be easily seen where these were built, as sufficient names are inserted for the comparison to be made.

Perhaps enough has been said to show what a big undertaking the drainage of the Fens has been. One other point, however, cannot be omitted. When the rivers are banked and canals and drains cut, there is still left the important item of lifting the water that collects in the drains into the rivers, so that it can find its way to the sea. This was accomplished by windmills. These were simple in construction, and so long as the wind blew at the right time they performed their work fairly satisfactorily. In an account of the river Ouse published in 1794 we read "There are fourteen mills on the west side and thirteen on the east side for draining the fens into the Ouse between Denver Sluice and Littleport Bridge, a distance of nine and a half miles". Most people put the old-fashioned windmill into their imaginative pictures of the Fens, but to-day it has been replaced by the more reliable steam-pumping apparatus, which does its work at the critical time even if the wind does not blow.

To the geography student the history of the Ouse and the drainage of the Fens afford an excellent illustration of the necessity of the control of river waters, a matter that to-day is becoming of prime importance. Rivers, when under control, are good servants of man, but such rivers as the Great Ouse, when uncontrolled, are bad masters. The Ouse Drainage Board are responsible for the management of the river, and their task is no light one.

The Fens have provided man with many other problems in his utilisation of the area. The sites of towns and villages, the size and boundaries of the parishes, the size and products of the farms, the direction and upkeep of the high roads and the construction of railways are all expressions of the nature of the country, and even when the full account of the history of the town of Cambridge comes to be written, it will be found that its situation and its site, its growth and its fame, have been controlled to some degree by the Fens.

THE ART THEATRE MOVEMENT

by TERENCE GRAY

I. HISTORY

Rebirths

THE renaissance of the theatre has spread throughout Europe. Like the renaissance of classical learning in the fifteenth century, it first manifested itself far from these shores, and was in Southern Europe an accomplished fact before it had seriously begun to affect the culture of these islands. As the cultured people of the Italian city-states in the fifteenth century looked upon the English of their day as rude barbarians, so—theatrically—do the cultured Germans, Czechs, and other Central European peoples look upon the English of our time. But now, as then, the balance is fast righting itself, and as then the Renaissance, when it did reach these shores, produced here some of the supreme achievements of the whole culture, so now we may hope and believe that the revitalised English theatre ultimately may contribute some of the best work of the movement.

In any great international renaissance each nation to some extent re-enacts within its own confines the evolution of the process as a whole. Alone England might never have succeeded in reconstituting her theatre, but the need and the impulse, though insufficiently potent, were there and were constantly manifest. The foreign germ created the fever which eventually stimulated the people of this country to activity, but the movement can be traced here as clearly and as independently as in the countries of its earliest achievement.

The Old Drama

The drama virtually died with the extinction of classical civilisation. Such survival as it had in the Middle Ages was confined on the one hand to vagrant poets and entertainers and, on the other, to religious representations. Its re-emergence coincided with, and indeed was a direct product of, the revival of classical learning in the Renaissance. But the form in which it was reborn was not purely classical. It represented a classical impulse applied to a medieval and racially evolved technique, the technique of the mystery plays and religious representations. But it was the classical impulse that got the job done and the classical impulse persisted, the two theatrical inheritances fusing into the hybrid Elizabethan drama of England, in which the medieval technique predominated, and the theatre of Racine and Corneille in France, in which the classical attained the ascendancy.

The Architectural Medium

Although the Elizabethan drama of England retained the native form and developed it into the theatre of Shakespeare with its multiplication of scenes, while the French theatre, moulded on the Hellenic form with its unity of scene and construction, took over the classical tradition, the two theatres converged in course of time, and the typical architecture of the one, that of the old

Elizabethan playhouse, was submerged as completely as was the Hellenic architecture which was the natural medium of the other.

The architectural result of the merging of these traditions was the playhouse which has descended to us from Georgian times and which the modern *trade theatre* has only adapted to the extent of enlarging the balconies out over the pit in order to increase the possible box-office receipts for the given area of the building.

In tracing the origin of the art theatre movement (often most ineptly called the "repertory" theatre movement) the two vital factors are the drama itself and its architectural medium, the playhouse in which it was performed. Naturally these two factors are interdependent, since the latter was evolved as the medium of the former, but it is necessary that each should be considered separately. The native drama, with its loose episodic construction, had its own typical architectural medium as exemplified later in the Elizabethan playhouse, which was evolved from performances in the courtyards of inns and castles. This architectural medium was admirably adapted for the performance of the plays which were given in it, as might be expected since that medium was specially evolved for that specific purpose and since those plays were specially constructed for performance in that specific medium. Apart from the Elizabethan playhouse, the native drama was admirably suited for performance in such native surroundings as a Gothic cathedral. This also was to be expected, since the native drama, as has been said, had developed from mystery plays and religious representations which had been devised for performance in churches, and moreover the loose construction, the episodic character, and the essential pageantry of the works lent themselves to performance in great architectural surroundings such as cathedrals, halls, courts, and public buildings.

The classical drama, on the other hand, demanded its own typical architectural medium, that medium which had been evolved for the specific purpose when classical drama itself first came into being; and the French and Italian pseudo-classical drama only demanded a modification of that medium in so far as its "pseudo" character departed from the purity of the original.

The fusion of the two traditions produced the playhouse which has come down to us and which is exemplified in the modern *trade theatre*.

The Dramatic Cycle

Leaving architecture for a moment and returning to drama itself, we have seen that the vitalising effect of the Renaissance of classical learning in the fifteenth century produced the dramatic renaissance which burgeoned in Elizabethan and contemporary continental drama. This fusion of native and classical traditions continued to bear fruit in irregular cycles of dramatic activity, descending in the scale of inspiration through Restoration times down to Georgian and Victorian, manifesting a final rally in the artificial creations of the school of Sardou. Thenceforth the English theatre was virtually dead, the vitalising force had expended itself, the last echo of the original inspiration had died away. It was with drama as with other things; civilisation itself, all manifestations of culture follow the same course. Such drama as survived was like all art at such periods in the cycle of culture, like Egypt in the Alexandrine period, like Rome after the Antonines. Drama continued, still continues, endlessly re-creating stale forms, concerned with trivialities, bounded by dead conventions, degraded to a trade level, and exploited for popular amusement by financial speculators.

II. THE ORIGIN OF THE NEW DRAMA

The "Repertory" System

This state of affairs was soon manifest to the vision of enlightened people, to people who could intellectually rise above the atmosphere of their own time. Such expression as they gave to their realisation of this state of affairs is the ultimate origin of the movement which became known as the "repertory" theatre movement. This name originates from an incidental rather than from an essential circumstance. At the time when the reaction first began to make itself felt in this country the old stock-company system had almost died out. The theatre had drifted into the hands of actor-managers who produced plays, largely for their own glorification as actors, for long runs or for provincial tours. On the continent, however, where the theatre was subsidised and administered by the State, the ancient system of a stock-company performing a large repertory of plays in rotation had survived, and to the first adherents of the movement this factor, which at most was responsible for a minor and local degeneration in the standard of performance, appeared the vital source of degeneracy. Accordingly they devoted themselves to restoring what has ever since been called the "repertory" system.

Their efforts had little success. They have never succeeded in restoring the repertory system. Probably they never will succeed, because the system is in many ways unsuited to modern theatrical conditions; but they founded the art theatre movement, they laid the foundations of the present renaissance of the Theatre as an Art, and their infernally ugly, foreign, and inept name has descended upon us as a dubious heritage from their worthy activities in the cause of drama. Actually the term "repertory" is now definitely applied to something that is not repertory at all, viz. a revival of the stock-company performing a different play every week or fortnight and repeating an outstanding success once every couple of years.

The "Naturalists"

Meanwhile on the continent, where theatres were State-supported, a new school of drama developed. This school, of which Ibsen became the prototype, represented a reaction and brought the theatre back into intimate contact with life by means of a fanatical exploitation of Realism.

In England, where the theatre was exclusively a private commercial enterprise in the hands of uncultured financiers, or of actors who had been from childhood too deep in the atmosphere of the traditional theatre to see the wood for the trees, the new school of Realism made no progress as far as public performance was concerned.

In the course of time, however, through the

channels of printed literature, the movement spread to this country, and men of genius arose, such as Mr Shaw, who wrote plays that could rank with the best work of Ibsen, Strindberg, and the continental dramatists. But performance of them there was none. As the supply increased, so did a demand begin to arise, but for decades it was too scattered and too intellectual to penetrate the barriers of the theatre-exploiters and hide-bound actor-managers.

At last the efforts of desperate and enlightened individuals produced sporadic performances and early repertory enterprises, but, one and all, these proved commercially impracticable. But the supply of real plays, British and foreign, piled up and piled up, the press began turning them out as printed literature, and the demand gradually spread and became more and more insistent. Finally the *trade theatres* overreached themselves. Their hide-bound obtuseness, their insular and unimaginative thick-headedness, brought the old-established theatre to its death-bed as the home of drama. Its prolonged refusal brought about its own downfall. The public arose and started to create its own theatre.

The Amateur Revival

The art theatre movement is essentially an amateur enterprise. Among amateurs it started, and those " repertory " theatres which are ashamed of their origin and seek to deny their amateur status are denying their birthright. Those which have imagination and understand what they are doing are proud of their ancestry and firmly assert their amateur status, for the fact that the more successful and prosperous are able to pay their actors and conduct their work as a sound commercial undertaking does not in any sense affiliate them to the old professional theatre, which has failed in its duty to society and to the drama, and which, but for the desperate enterprise of the amateurs, would have allowed the theatre as an art to disappear from the face of the earth for ever. The prosperity of the new art theatre movement demands that those who practise it shall adhere whole-heartedly to the great amateur spirit which gave it birth, and the largest and most successful companies must realise that they are racially more akin to the small amateur village enterprises than to the decadent and futile *trade theatre* with whom their only kinship is the incidental matter of payment for services.

The Art and the Trade Theatres

The essential cleavage between the art and trade theatres, though it may appear to narrow in the direction of financial organisation and a certain mutual interchange of artists and craftsmen, will assuredly widen. The more successful art theatres are learning by experience that it is in their best interests to train up their own actors, producers, designers, and workers rather than to hire those who have grown up in the trade theatre, and the best artists whom these larger art theatres have brought to the front have almost always been men and women whom they have taken originally from the amateur ranks. A certain interchange there will always be. Artists who have attained proficiency with the art theatres will go over to the trade theatres as long as the trade theatres can hold out larger financial rewards, and genuine artists who have started their career in the trade theatre will go over to the art theatres when they find conditions in the former fail to give scope to their artistic impulses.

Another factor which tends superficially to merge the two opposing types of endeavour is that they were in the past, and largely are at present, obliged to share an architectural medium. Small art-theatre companies, without resources, commence operations in local halls and available public buildings. Later, with success, they aspire to hiring or permanently acquiring cheap and sometimes dilapidated ancient playhouses. Unable to raise funds, except in America, sufficient to build theatres for themselves, they seek to carry out their work in the homes of the trade theatre. This brings my analysis to its final stage.

The Death-bed of the Renaissance

While England has been fighting to secure public performances of the accumulation of several decades of genuine drama based on the Ibsenite naturalistic reaction, the continental dramatists with their State-supported theatres have lived through that phase and exploited its possibilities. The artistic and cultural exhaustion which manifested itself here in the late Victorian and Edwardian periods, which produced practically no art or craft of value that definitely belonged to and expressed its own day, which endlessly and basely went on reproducing antique forms in furniture and every necessity of life, which came to regard everything ancient as beautiful and valuable, and everything modern (rightly enough) as ugly and valueless, brought the old artistic tradition, which had originated in the Renaissance (which, as I have explained, caused native art-forms to burgeon and blossom by means of the vitalising classical admixture), to a final and absolute FULL STOP. Henceforth the Renaissance culture was DEAD. It survived—it still survives—in mechanical reproduction, but as a vital creative impulse it finally petered out.

The New Art

The land lay fallow for a while, but the present renaissance began in Central Europe and commenced to bud before it was even suspected in these islands. Even to-day, when the new art-forms are everywhere in Northern and Central Europe, when the great Paris exhibition of 1925, devoted exclusively to modern art in all its forms, is nearly three years in the past, the living art of the present day is barely known to exist in this country and is still regarded by most of those who have seen examples of it as "ugly" and the pastime of eccentric persons who are assumed to live in Chelsea.

However that may be, the post-war world has found an artistic rebirth. It has found a means of self-expression. In architecture, in painting, sculpture, furniture, decoration, all the handicrafts, the theatre, and all other media in which the human mind finds expression in art, new methods, new forms, new inspirations are bursting into life.

The new Art of the Theatre, born more than a decade ago abroad, flourishing, widely understood, practised and appreciated in Central Europe, almost mature in many cities, is just beginning to be understood and practised in England.

The New Drama

This new Art of the Theatre owes little, save experience, to the old Renaissance culture, owes nothing in inspiration, ranks Egypt and China as high artistically, if not higher, than Greece, and has broken down the literary bondage of the old theatre. The written text of a play is to it but a component part, an important, a vital, but not the ubiquitous part, of a composite whole which is the Art of the Theatre. Author, as ultimate creator, remains—must remain—supreme, but he now has at his command a vastly increased medium of expression. The spoken word is but one element among others, of which the most important are Movement (dancing, expression by gesture, crowd-movement), Lighting (colour, expression by atmo-sphere, scenic and decorative projection), Paint-ing (pictorial and decorative expression by means of pigment), Architecture (form, emotional ex-pression by means of planes and mass), Sculpture (expression outside the limited range attainable by the human face and body, through masks and lay figures), Sound (music, emotional expression by means of audile devices, repetition, recurrence, crescendo of natural and artificial noise forma-tions), and the as yet barely attempted use of the sense of Smell. All these are in varying but still elementary stages of evolution as parts of the composite Art of the Theatre, and each requires its own specialised craftsmen to carry out the author's conception under the direction of the producer.

The New Playhouse

Almost needless to say, this new composite Art of the Theatre needs an architectural medium far removed from the old Renaissance-inspired trade-theatre playhouse. In fact it is not in any way possible adequately to practise it in the old theatre buildings. But the old "repertory" movement in England, always somewhat isolated and out of touch with the continental development of the essentially same movement, lacks both money and initiative to bring English endeavour to the front. Most of all it lacks vision. It is isolated, its own members are isolated even from one another, its right hand does not know what its left has just been doing. It does not see or profit by its neighbours' successful and unsuccessful experiments. It has no co-operation and little desire for co-operation. But for the welling-up of interest in the intelligent section of the public, it would die from its own isolated sterility. But little as the new art of our own day is practised in this country at present, the impulse which brought it to fruition abroad is manifest among our people as a whole, and their developing craving will bring about a closer co-operation and a renewed phase of enterprise and development in the *art theatre* movement.

But before anything vital can be done, before England can hope to contribute anything of permanent value to the movement, the architectural medium must be developed and perfected. In this the cleavage from the old trade theatre will be complete.

The Lonely Island

England is pitiful in its artistic isolation. The clash of ideas on the continent strikes fire into such movements from Bergen to Madrid, from Danzig to Rome, from Amsterdam to Sofia. But England plays a lone hand, seeking by its own labouring instinct to achieve something independently, not from pride or conceit, but from sheer insulation and ignorance. England is like a domestic electric-lamp flex running beside a great power-cable but insulated from it and oblivious of it through the interposition of a little intervening Channel. The pitiful compromise, when there is any trace at all of the developments long accepted and well-nigh perfected elsewhere, evidenced in worthy national undertakings such as the rebuilding of the Stratford Memorial Theatre or in small private dramatic enterprises, is a disheartening reminder of what work remains for men of the theatre who understand and have vision, before England can hope to come abreast of current achievement elsewhere.

New Wine in Old Bottles

But the failure of examples of genuine drama in the trade-theatre playhouses, on the rare occasions when bold financiers have allowed themselves half-heartedly to be jockeyed into trying the experiment of producing them, may largely and confidently be attributed to the fact that the trade-theatre playhouse was evolved for the performance of drawing-room comedy, social comedy, crook melodrama, all current forms of artificial, mechanically contrived entertainment, and is fundamentally unsuited either for the performance of vital natural drama or for the practice of any form of serious stagecraft as that term is understood in the Art of the Theatre. Neither Greek tragedy, Shakespearian drama, nor Expressionist drama of the modern school can ever adequately be performed in the trade-theatre playhouse.

The Theatre of the Future

All three require the new architectural medium, for that medium goes back basically to the Hellenic theatre and takes to itself the essential elements of the classical playhouse, which had fundamentally (though not in detail) the perfect auditorium, and incorporates the grandeur of the Gothic cathedral and the intimacy of the Elizabethan theatre, on which simple and eternal foundations it builds the new stage in which modern science provides the mechanical media of expression, a complicated instrument on which the Art of the Theatre of the future will play its great music.

ALPHABETICAL KEY TO PLAN
OF EXHIBITION

(see plan on opposite page)

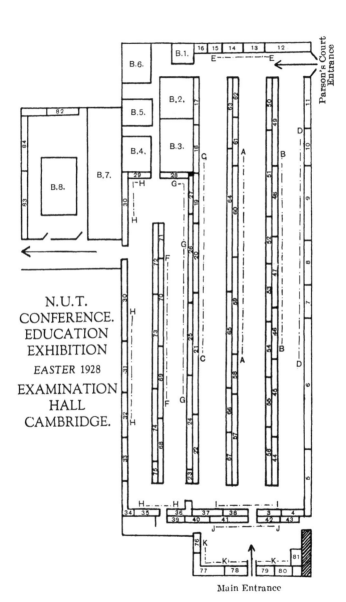

Parson's Court Entrance

N.U.T.
CONFERENCE.
EDUCATION
EXHIBITION
EASTER 1928
EXAMINATION
HALL
CAMBRIDGE.

Main Entrance

INDEX TO ADVERTISERS

METHUEN & CO., LTD.

Recent Books which should be inspected at STALL No. 29

Days and Ways of Early Man. By DOROTHY DAVISON. With 47 Illustrations. **2s. 6d.**; also Prize Edition, with a Coloured Frontispiece, **5s.** net.

Water Folk at the Zoo: A Book of the Aquarium. By GLADYS DAVIDSON, F.Z.S. With 23 Illustrations. **1s. 6d.**; also Prize Edition, with Coloured Frontispiece, **5s.** net.

Adventures among Words. By HENRY BRIERLEY, LL.D. **1s. 6d.**

Our England: Twelve Open-Air Lessons. By PATRICIA JOHNSON. With 10 Illustrations. **2s.**

⁂

ROSE FYLEMAN

The Rainbow Cat: and Other Stories. Limp Cloth, **1s. 6d.**

Forty Good-night Tales. Limp Cloth, **1s. 6d.**

⁂

With the Prince round the Empire. By CHARLES TURLEY. With 26 Illustrations and 4 Maps. **1s. 6d.** Prize Edition, **3s. 6d.** net.

An Introduction to Chemistry. By J. MORRIS, M.A. (Oxon.). With 49 Diagrams. **3s.**

Simple Art Crafts and Stage Craft for Schools. By FREDERICK GARNETT, A.S.A.M., A.M.C. With 62 Illustrations. Demy 4to. **3s.**

METHUEN'S MODERN CLASSICS
Cloth Boards, **1s. 6d.**

1. **The Wind in the Willows.** By KENNETH GRAHAME. 3rd Edition.
2. **The Blue Bird.** By MAURICE MAETERLINCK.
3. **White Fang.** By JACK LONDON. Abridged.
4. **Spanish Gold.** By GEORGE A. BIRMINGHAM. Abridged.
5. **Fifteen Stories.** By W. W. JACOBS.
6. **Milestones.** By ARNOLD BENNETT and EDWARD KNOBLOCK; and **The Great Adventure.** By ARNOLD BENNETT. In one Volume.
7. **Essays by Modern Masters.**
8. **Essays of a Naturalist.** By Sir RAY LANKESTER. Illustrated.
9. **The Gentlest Art.** An Anthology of English Letters. By E. V. LUCAS.

Open Sesame: An Anthology of English Poems for Children from Seven to Ten Years of Age. Compiled by J. COMPTON, M.A. Director of Education, Barking. 2nd Edition. **2s.**

The Curtain Rises. A Collection of Plays for young Readers and Actors. Made by J. COMPTON, M.A. **2s.**

The Study of Nature with Children. By M. G. CARTER, B.Sc. With 3 Diagrams. **3s. 6d.**

Practical Courses in Housecraft. Edited by EVELYN E. JARDINE, M.A., B.Sc. **3s. 6d.**

METHUEN & CO., LTD., 36 ESSEX STREET, LONDON, W.C. 2

Cassell's Noted School Books

STAND No. F 70 EXAMINATION HALLS

May we have the pleasure of your visit to Stall No. 70 where our Representatives (Messrs J. E. Wittrick, H. Evans, and George A. Weaver) will be glad to show you our books and to answer all enquiries.

A full range of Educational Books, Prize Books and Library Books will be found displayed on the Stall.

Messrs Cassell & Co. will be pleased to send to your address full particulars and specimen pages of any Educational Books.

They will also send at your request:

CASSELL'S SPRING (1928) LIST
CASSELL'S TECHNICAL BOOK LIST
CASSELL'S PRIZE BOOK LIST

CASSELL & Co. Ltd.
LA BELLE SAUVAGE

LUDGATE HILL
LONDON, E.C.4

iv

Sunshine Readers

Good clear type, delightful
coloured pictures, well bound

Sunshine Primers, NOS. 1 *and* 2   10d. & 1s.

Sunshine Infant Readers, NOS. 1 *and* 2   1s. 2d.

Sunshine Verses, A FIRST READER IN VERSE   1s.

Sunshine Readers, NOS. 1, 2 *and* 3
                                    1s. 8d., 1s. 10d., 2s.

Sunshine Bible Readers, NOS. 1 *and* 2   1s. 9d.
                          NOS. 3 *and* 4   2s.

———————❖———————

Nation Primer, NO. 1   9d.

Nation Story Readers, 16 TITLES   6d. to 9d.

Bouverie Historical Stories, 4 TITLES   1s. 6d.

Nature Books.   The R.T.S. publish a large range
of Nature Books, well written,
beautifully illustrated, accurate
and reliable.

Pictures.   The R.T.S. has a wonderful collection of Pictures suitable for
teaching purposes.

LISTS & SPECIMENS ON APPLICATION

THE RELIGIOUS TRACT SOCIETY

4 Bouverie Street, London, E.C. 4

OXFORD BOOKS

THE following series have established themselves firmly among the best and most popular school books:

> **Constructive English**
>
> **Oxford Reading Books**
>
> **Herbert Strang's Readers**
>
> **Mrs Strang's Readers**
>
> **Herbert Strang's Library**
>
> **New World Geographies**

FULL PARTICULARS
will be sent
ON APPLICATION

Oxford University Press
FALCON SQUARE, LONDON, E.C.1

WHY NOT A DELIGHTFUL
Sea Trip Holiday

—enjoy the thrill of a voyage across the Atlantic in a great White Star Liner, amid comfort and congeniality and opportunity for healthful recreation, including sports, music and dancing,

with a Tour in
U.S.A. & CANADA

including visits to world renowned Cities and famed Niagara Falls. A memorable holiday of about Three weeks at surprisingly moderate cost

FROM

TOURIST
THIRD CABIN **£38** RETURN
OCEAN FARE

(including an excellent Cuisine)

TOURS ARRANGED

WHITE STAR

BOOKS

A Bookshop should be a place where you go regularly, not so much to buy books, but to find out what has been happening in the realm of thought and literature. We invite you into our establishment to look round at your leisure. Our assistants are there to answer your queries and to assist you in every way.

4 PETTY CURY

STATIONERY

The ideal Stationery shop must not only keep a stock of writing requisites but also an infinitely varied selection of attractive little things, fancy goods, pictures, books, games, artists' materials, and those hundred and one things for the pocket and the desk that we all love. We invite you to visit our shop at

18 and 19 SIDNEY STREET

W. HEFFER & SONS, Ltd.
CAMBRIDGE

BOOKSELLERS, PUBLISHERS, STATIONERS & PRINTERS

Telephone 862

NATIONAL SAVINGS MOVEMENT

THERE are over 16,000 School Savings Associations.

Savings Associations are clubs for the easy purchase of Savings Certificates by small instalments. Savings Certificates are the best investment for small savings. For a full explanation of how to run a School Savings Association, you are invited to apply to

The National Savings Committee's STALL **E16**

NATIONAL UNION of TEACHERS EDUCATION EXHIBITION

or to

the Committee's Headquarters, Sanctuary Buildings, Gt. Smith Street, London, S.W.1

An Historic Bookshop

(ESTABLISHED OVER 340 YEARS)

∽

SINCE 1581, and possibly earlier, No. 1 Trinity Street has been known to successive generations of Undergraduates and others in Cambridge as a resort for book-lovers.

IT is still a centre for those who seek good Literature, both new and old, and working books in all subjects.

FOREIGN BOOKS may be seen in large numbers or obtained promptly from abroad.

∽

The Bookshop opposite the Senate House

BOWES AND BOWES

1 & 2 TRINITY STREET, CAMBRIDGE

After the Conference—

By Royal Appointment
His Majesty The King

See specimens of "Dusmo-cleaned" school floors at Stand B 46, National Union of Teachers Conference.

ACTION!

NONE of the progressive reforms discussed at the Conference can be really effective unless the standard of health amongst scholars is first put right.

Ill-health is very largely due to the spreading of germs—germs which lurk and breed in dust. The old methods of cleaning do not settle the question of dust; they only RAISE it—and disperse it about the building.

The one way to have real, germ-free cleanliness is by using the modern, scientific "Dusmo" Method.

As "Dusmo" is swept in a line across the floor, it *absorbs* the dust and *kills* the germs—and gradually gives the floor a smooth, clean sheen.

METHOD

This method or that method? Which?

This is for ever *the* question among members of the Scholastic Profession.

The Method that seeks to co-operate with the Teacher and which has convinced 42 countries of the world as the best for making character in boys is Scouting for Boys.

May we send you particulars? Write The Secretary, Room C.S. Boy Scouts Association, 25 Buckingham Palace Road, London, S.W.1

See THE MODEL CAMP *in Publishers' Exhibition*

9 781107 494435